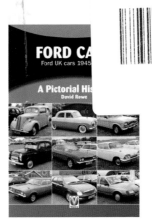

FORD CA
Ford UK cars 1945

A Pictorial His
David Rowe

CW00751377

VELOCE PUBLISHING
THE PUBLISHER OF FINE AUTOMOTIVE BOOKS

Enthusiast's Restoration Manual
Series
Citroën 2CV Restore (Porter)
Classic British Car Electrical Systems
  (Astley)
Classic Car Bodywork, How to
  Restore (Thaddeus)
Classic Car Electrics (Thaddeus)
Classic Car Suspension, Steering &
  Wheels, How to Restore & Improve
  (Parish – translator)
Classic Cars, How to Paint
  (Thaddeus)
Classic Off-road Motorcycles, How to
  Jaguar E-type (Crespin)
Reliant Regal, How to Restore
  (Payne)
Triumph TR2, 3, 3A, 4 & 4A, How to
  Restore (Williams)
Triumph TR5/250 & 6, How to
  Restore (Williams)
Triumph TR7/8, How to Restore
  (Williams)
Ultimate Mini Restoration Manual,
  The (Ayre & Webber)
Volkswagen Beetle, How to Restore
  (Tyler)
VW Bay Window Bus (Paxton)

A Pictorial History Series
Austin Cars 1948 to 1990 – A Pictorial
  History (Rowe)
Ford Cars (UK) – A Pictorial History
  (Rowe)
Morris Cars – 1948-1984 (Newell)
Rootes Cars of the 50s, 60s & 70s –
  Hillman, Humber, Singer, Sunbeam
  & Talbot, A Pictorial History (Rowe)
Rover Cars 1945 to 2005 – A Pictorial
  History (Taylor)
Triumph & Standard Cars 1945
  to 1984 – A Pictorial History
  (Warrington)
Wolseley Cars 1948 to 1975 – A
  Pictorial History (Rowe)

Expert Guides
Land Rover Series I-III – Your expert
  guide to common problems & how
  to fix them (Thurman)
MG Midget & A-H Sprite – Your expert
  guide to common problems & how
  to fix them (Horler)
Triumph TR4 & TR4A – Your expert
  guide to common problems & how
  to fix them (Hogan)
Triumph TR6 – Your expert guide
  to common problems & how to fix
  them (Hogan)

Essential Buyer's Guide Series
Alfa Romeo Alfasud (Metcalfe)
Alfa Romeo Alfetta: all saloon/sedan
  models 1972 to 1984 & coupé
  models 1974 to 1987 (Metcalfe)
Alfa Romeo Giulia GT Coupé
  (Booker)
Alfa Romeo Giulia Spider (Booker)
Audi TT (Davies)
Audi TT Mk2 2006 to 2014 (Durnan)
Austin-Healey Big Healeys (Trummel)
BMW Boxer Twins (Henshaw)
BMW E30 3 Series 1981 to 1994
  (Hosier)
BMW GS (Henshaw)
BMW X5 (Saunders)
BMW Z3 Roadster (Fishwick)
BMW Z4: E85 Roadster and E86
  Coupé including M and Alpina 2003
  to 2009 (Smitheram)
BSA 350, 441 & 500 Singles
  (Henshaw)
BSA 500 & 650 Twins (Henshaw)
BSA Bantam (Henshaw)
Choosing, Using & Maintaining Your
  Electric Bicycle (Henshaw)
Citroën 2CV (Paxton)
Citroën DS & ID (Heilig)
Cobra Replicas (Ayre)

Corvette C2 Sting Ray 1963-1967
  (Falconer)
Datsun 240Z 1969 to 1973 (Newlyn)
DeLorean DMC-12 1981 to 1983
  (Williams)
Ducati Bevel Twins (Falloon)
Ducati Desmodue Twins (Falloon)
Ducati Desmoquattro Twins – 851,
  888, 916, 996, 998, ST4 1988 to
  2004 (Falloon)
Fiat 500 & 600 (Bobbitt)
Ford Capri (Paxton)
Ford Escort Mk1 & Mk2 (Williamson)
Ford Focus RS/ST 1st Generation
  (Williamson)
Ford Model A – All Models 1927 to
  1931 (Buckley)
Ford Model T – All models 1909 to
  1927 (Barker)
Ford Mustang – First Generation
  1964 to 1973 (Cook)
Ford Mustang – Fifth Generation
  (2005-2014) (Cook)
Ford RS Cosworth Sierra & Escort
  (Williamson)
Harley-Davidson Big Twins
  (Henshaw)
Hillman Imp (Morgan)
Hinckley Triumph triples & fours 750,
  900, 955, 1000, 1050, 1200 – 1991-
  2009 (Henshaw)
Honda CBR FireBlade (Henshaw)
Honda CBR600 Hurricane (Henshaw)
Honda SOHC Fours 1969-1984
  (Henshaw)
Jaguar E-Type 3.8 & 4.2 litre
  (Crespin)
Jaguar E-type V12 5.3 litre (Crespin)
Jaguar Mark 1 & 2 (All models
  including Daimler 2.5-litre V8) 1955
  to 1969 (Thorley)
Jaguar New XK 2005-2014 (Thorley)
Jaguar S-Type – 1999 to 2007
  (Thorley)
Jaguar X-Type – 2001 to 2009
  (Thorley)
Jaguar XJ-S (Crespin)
Jaguar XJ6, XJ8 & XJR (Thorley)
Jaguar XK 120, 140 & 150 (Thorley)
Jaguar XK8 & XKR (1996-2005)
  (Thorley)
Jaguar/Daimler XJ 1994-2003
  (Crespin)
Jaguar/Daimler XJ40 (Crespin)
Jaguar/Daimler XJ6, XJ12 &
  Sovereign (Crespin)
Kawasaki Z1 & Z900 (Orritt)
Land Rover Discovery Series 1
  (1989-1998) (Taylor)
Land Rover Discovery Series 2
  (1998-2004) (Taylor)
Land Rover Series I, II & IIA
  (Thurman)
Land Rover Series III (Thurman)
Lotus Elan, S1 to Sprint and Plus 2 to
  Plus 2S 130/5 1962 to 1974 (Vale)
Lotus Europa, S1, S2, Twin-cam &
  Special 1966 to 1975 (Vale)
Lotus Seven replicas & Caterham 7:
  1973-2013 (Hawkins)
Mazda MX-5 Miata (Mk1 1989-97 &
  Mk2 98-2001) (Crook)
Mazda RX-8 (Parish)
Mercedes-Benz 190: all 190 models
  (W201 series) 1982 to 1993 (Parish)
Mercedes-Benz 280-560SL & SLC
  (Bass)
Mercedes-Benz G-Wagen (Greene)
Mercedes-Benz Pagoda 230SL,
  250SL & 280SL roadsters & coupés
  (Bass)
Mercedes-Benz S-Class W126 Series
  (Zoporowski)
Mercedes-Benz S-Class Second
  Generation W116 Series (Parish)
Mercedes-Benz SL R129-series 1989
  to 2001 (Parish)
Mercedes-Benz SLK (Bass)
Mercedes-Benz W123 (Parish)

Mercedes-Benz W124 – All models
  1984-1997 (Zoporowski)
MG Midget & A-H Sprite (Horler)
MG TD, TF & TF1500 (Jones)
MGA 1955-1962 (Crosier)
MGB & MGB GT (Williams)
MGF & MG TF (Hawkins)
Mini (Paxton)
Morgan Plus 4 (Benfield)
Morris Minor & 1000 (Newell)
Moto Guzzi 2-valve big twins
  (Falloon)
New Mini (Collins)
Norton Commando (Henshaw)
Peugeot 205 GTI (Blackburn)
Piaggio Scooters – all modern two-
  stroke & four-stroke automatic
  models 1991 to 2016 (Willis)
Porsche 356 (Johnson)
Porsche 911 (964) (Streather)
Porsche 911 (991) (Streather)
Porsche 911 (993) (Streather)
Porsche 911 (996) (Streather)
Porsche 911 (997) – Model years
  2004 to 2009 (Streather)
Porsche 911 (997) – Second
  generation models 2009 to 2012
  (Streather)
Porsche 911 Carrera 3.2 (Streather)
Porsche 911SC (Streather)
Porsche 924 – All models 1976 to
  1988 (Hodgkins)
Porsche 928 (Hemmings)
Porsche 930 Turbo & 911 (930) Turbo
  (Streather)
Porsche 944 (Higgins)
Porsche 981 Boxster & Cayman
  (Streather)
Porsche 986 Boxster (Streather)
Porsche 987 Boxster and Cayman 1st
  generation (2005-2009) (Streather)
Porsche 987 Boxster and Cayman
  2nd generation (2009-2012)
  (Streather)
Range Rover – First Generation
  models 1970 to 1996 (Taylor)
Range Rover – Second Generation
  1994-2001 (Taylor)
Range Rover – Third Generation
  L322 (2002-2012) (Taylor)
Reliant Scimitar GTE (Payne)
Rolls-Royce Silver Shadow & Bentley
  T-Series (Bobbitt)
Rover 2000, 2200 & 3500 (Marrocco)
Royal Enfield Bullet (Henshaw)
Subaru Impreza (Hobbs)
Sunbeam Alpine (Barker)
Triumph 350 & 500 Twins (Henshaw)
Triumph Bonneville (Henshaw)
Triumph Herald & Vitesse (Ayre)
Triumph Spitfire and GT6 (Ayre)
Triumph Stag (Mort)
Triumph Thunderbird, Trophy & Tiger
  (Henshaw)
Triumph TR2 & TR3 – All models
  (including 3A & 3B) 1953 to 1962
  (Conners)
Triumph TR4/4A & TR5/250 - All
  models 1961 to 1968 (Child &
  Battyll)
Triumph TR6 (Williams)
Triumph TR7 & TR8 (Williams)
Triumph Trident & BSA Rocket III
  (Rooke)
TVR Chimaera and Griffith (Kitchen)
TVR S-series (Kitchen)
Velocette 350 & 500 Singles 1946 to
  1970 (Henshaw)
Vespa Scooters – Classic 2-stroke
  models 1960-2008 (Paxton)
Volkswagen Bus (Copping)
Volkswagen Transporter T4 (1990-
  2003) (Copping/Cservenka)
VW Golf GTI (Copping)
VW Beetle (Copping)
Volvo 700/900 Series (Beavis)
Volvo P1800/1800S, E & ES 1961 to
  1973 (Murray)

Those Were The Days ... Series
Alpine Trials & Rallies 1910-1973
  (Pfundner)
American 1/2-ton Pickup Trucks of the
  1950s (Mort)
American 1/2-ton Pickup Trucks of the
  1960s (Mort)
American 'Independent' Automakers –
  AMC to Willys 1945 to 1960 (Mort)
American Station Wagons – The
  Golden Era 1950-1975 (Mort)
American Trucks of the 1950s (Mort)
American Trucks of the 1960s (Mort)
American Woodies 1928-1953 (Mort)
Anglo-American Cars from the 1930s
  to the 1970s (Mort)
Austerity Motoring (Bobbitt)
Austins, The last real (Peck)
Brighton National Speed Trials
  (Gardiner)
British and European Trucks of the
  1970s (Peck)
British Drag Racing – The early
  years (Pettitt)
British Lorries of the 1950s (Bobbitt)
British Lorries of the 1960s (Bobbitt)
British Touring Car Racing (Collins)
British Police Cars (Walker)
British Woodies (Peck)
Buick Riviera (Mort)
Café Racer Phenomenon, The
  (Walker)
Chevrolet ½-ton C/K-Series Pickup
  Trucks 1973-1987 (Mort)
Don Hayter's MGB Story – The birth
  of the MGB in MG's Abingdon
  Design & Development Office
  (Hayter)
Drag Bike Racing in Britain – From
  the mid '60s to the mid '80s (Lee)
Dune Buggy Phenomenon, The
  (Hale)
Dune Buggy Phenomenon Volume
  2, The (Hale)
Endurance Racing at Silverstone in
  the 1970s & 1980s (Parker)
Hot Rod & Stock Car Racing in Britain
  in the 1980s (Neil)
Mercedes-Benz Trucks (Peck)
MG's Abingdon Factory (Moylan)
Motor Racing at Brands Hatch in the
  Seventies (Parker)
Motor Racing at Brands Hatch in the
  Eighties (Parker)
Motor Racing at Crystal Palace
  (Collins)
Motor Racing at Goodwood in the
  Sixties (Gardiner)
Motor Racing at Nassau in the 1950s
  & 1960s (O'Neil)
Motor Racing at Oulton Park in the
  1960s (McFadyen)
Motor Racing at Oulton Park in the
  1970s (McFadyen)
Motor Racing at Thruxton in the
  1970s (Grant-Braham)
Motor Racing at Thruxton in the
  1980s (Grant-Braham)
Superprix – The Story of Birmingham
  Motor Race (Page & Collins)
Three Wheelers (Bobbitt)

Great Cars
Austin-Healey – A celebration of the
  fabulous 'Big' Healey (Piggott)
Jaguar E-type (Thorley)
Jaguar Mark 1 & 2 (Thorley)
Jaguar XK A Celebration of Jaguar's
  1950s Classic (Thorley)
Triumph TR – TR2 to 6: The last of
  the traditional sports cars (Piggott)
Volkswagen Beetle – A Celebration
  of the World's Most Popular Car
  (Copping)

www.veloce.co.uk

First published in April 2021 by Veloce Publishing Limited, Veloce House, Parkway Farm Business Park, Middle Farm Way, Poundbury, Dorchester DT1 3AR, England.
Tel +44 (0)1305 260068 / Fax 01305 250479 / e-mail info@veloce.co.uk / web www.veloce.co.uk or www.velocebooks.com.
ISBN:978-1-787116-42-9; UPC: 6-36847-01642-5.

FORD CARS
Ford UK cars 1945-1995

A Pictorial History
David Rowe

VELOCE

CONTENTS

A history of Ford in the UK

Ford Motor Company (England) Limited was founded in 1910 to handle the import of cars from the USA. The actual assembly of the Model T cars commenced in 1911 at an old tramworks in Trafford Park, Manchester, near the Manchester Ship Canal. This proximity to the canal meant that the cars could be delivered direct to the factory without needing to be unloaded at Liverpool docks and then transferred onwards. There was also a railway siding near the factory so that cars could be distributed to dealers across the country.

Initially, the cars shipped to Manchester had almost all components manufactured in the USA. Gradually, though, parts began to be produced locally. Ford's purpose-built factory in Dagenham, Essex, opened on 1st October 1931, by which time the Model A had replaced the T. However, with the American-designed cars being penalised by the horsepower tax based on engine bore, and more modern cars appearing from the likes of Austin and Morris, the decision was taken to produce cars in the UK that were better suited to the European marketplace. Thus the Model Y, with its 933cc sidevalve engine rated at 8hp, was introduced. Then, in 1934, the Model C, with a 1172cc engine rated at 10hp, was introduced. It was only with the introduction of the 7W Ten in 1937, which subsequently evolved into the

This photograph was taken outside the author's house in 1999. Members of his family have owned a number of Escorts and other Ford models over many years, and the author, who has worked as an accountant at two Ford dealerships, has driven over 100 Fords.

affectionately named 'sit up and beg' Anglia and Prefect models, that the styling of cars was largely left to British designers.

Production of some V8-engined cars did continue for a while, the last of which, the V8 Pilot, being discontinued in 1951; by which time the Ford Zephyr had taken over as Ford's big car.

Ford had encouraged some of its suppliers to set up factories alongside its Dagenham plant. These were eventually absorbed by Ford, however, which also acquired a disused factory in Langley, Berkshire, for use as a parts depot. Langley was also used for the production of Ford's commercial vehicles, but the Transit van's success ultimately led to its production being relocated to Southampton.

The Transit was the result of collaboration between Britain and Germany, and signalled the start of the creation of Ford Europe, with a single range of vehicles replacing locally designed and built models. It would also ultimately lead to production of some vehicles previously built in the UK being transferred to factories across Europe.

In the 1950s, different countries produced cars of their own design, although Ford's design studio in the USA sometimes had an influence after plans had been submitted for approval. There were certain similarities between the curved styling of the Taunus of Germany and the Zephyr mark 1 of England,

for example, but with the arrival of the Ford Anglia 105E in 1959, with its reverse raked rear screen, there was nothing else produced by Ford's factories in Europe that bore any resemblance to this uniquely British model (perhaps most well known these days due to its appearance in the Harry Potter films). The Consul Classic also had this style of rear window, and the coupé version of this car carried a name that would ultimately be applied to a car manufactured and sold throughout Europe: the Capri.

The Corsair, introduced in 1963 to replace the Classic, bore a certain resemblance to the US Ford Thunderbird. The Corsair, which inherited some of the Classic's components, such as its engine, was the first Ford to be produced at the Halewood factory in Liverpool. With Britain and Germany competing for world markets, there was a certain amount of rivalry between the two, highlighted by an attempt at one-upmanship by the British design studio when choosing a codename for the Cortina mark 1, a direct competitor to the 1960s Taunus. However, by 1968, both countries were producing identical cars, with the Escort being followed by the Capri in 1969. In 1970,

Pictured here are some of the vehicles that are not included in this book. These were subsequently introduced to enable Ford to compete within new markets as they emerged, such as MPVs (people carriers). Right: Ford Ka; below: Ford Galaxy.

though, with the launch of the Cortina mark 3, the two countries resorted to different designs of competing models, but then, following the introduction of the Cortina mark 4, and with the exception of Cortina or Taunus name badges, both countries were once again producing identical cars.

Although coupé versions of Taunus models were produced, there were never any Cortina coupés. Consideration was given to producing such a model based on the Cortina mark 1, and a prototype, called the Saxon, was built. Crayford Engineering converted some Cortina models into convertibles, and also produced Corsair and Capri convertibles.

Granada models were initially produced in England and Germany, albeit with different, locally produced engines (with the exception of diesel engines which, for all markets, were based on a Peugeot unit), but eventually the

British Granada adopted the same engines as used in Germany. Ultimately, all Granada production was transferred to Europe.

Bodies for the Fiesta, introduced in 1977, were produced at Valencia in Spain, but Ford factories in other countries were responsible for producing some of the car's components, with the engine blocks and radiators coming from Dagenham, transmissions from Bordeaux in France, and carburettors from Belfast. Final assembly of the Fiesta took place in several factories throughout Europe, including Dagenham.

With its Fiesta, Ford beat rival Vauxhall at producing its first front-wheel drive car (it was 1987 before Vauxhall launched its Fiesta competitor: the Nova). The first front-wheel drive Vauxhall was the Astra, introduced as a rival for the Ford Escort, which, following on from the Fiesta, switched to front-wheel drive in 1980. The Cortina replacement, the Sierra, launched in 1982, had rear-wheel drive, and it was not until the arrival of the Mondeo in 1993 that Ford committed to front-wheel drive for all its mainstream cars. Some Transit vans also switched to front-wheel drive in 2000.

After 30 years the Focus replaced the Escort.

Ford V8 Pilot

Introduced in August 1947, the Pilot was derived from the V8 62 model introduced in 1937 and discontinued in 1941. The Pilot was produced until May 1951, by which time its successor, the Ford Zephyr, had been around for over a year. The Pilot was the last UK Ford to feature a V8 (all further engines were four- or six-cylinder, usually in-line). The Ford Corsair, however, adopted a V4 in 1965, followed by the V6 fitted to Zephyr and Zodiac models in 1966. Standard equipment for the Pilot included a clock, heater, cigarette lighter, three ashtrays, twin horns, driver and passenger sun visors, arm rests on all doors, footrests, remote control rear window blind, and a built-in hydraulic jacking system to lift up the car and enable wheels to be changed. Optional extras included a radio and leather upholstery.

COLOURS: Black, Dark Blue, Beige, Light Green.
ENGINE: Eight-cylinder V formation, SV, bore 77.79mm, stroke 92.25mm, 3622cc (221.18in³), maximum bhp 85 at 3500rpm, Solex dual DD carburettor.
GEARBOX: Three-speed, synchromesh on top and intermediate gears, steering column gear change.

REAR AXLE: Spiral bevel, ratio 4.11:1.
BRAKES: Girling, front hydraulic, rear mechanical, drum brakes front and rear.
STEERING: Worm and sector.
TYRES: 6.00 x 16.
SUSPENSION: Transverse leaf springs, front anti-roll bar, hydraulic lever arm shock absorbers front and rear.
DIMENSIONS: Length: 14ft 6.75in (4.438m); **width**: 5ft 9.5in (1.765m); **height**: 5ft 6in (1.676m); **wheelbase**: 9ft 0.25in (2.75m); **track**: front 4ft 7.25in (1.403m), rear 4ft 10in (1.473m); **ground clearance**: 8.25in (21cm); **turning circle**: 42ft (12.77m).
APPROXIMATE WEIGHT: 1ton 8cwt 2qtr (1448kg).
CAPACITIES: Fuel 12.5 gallons (56.8 litres).

Ford Anglia E04, E494, Prefect E93, E493 and Popular 103E

Often referred to as the 'sit up and beg' cars, the Anglia and Prefect from 1945 onwards were essentially the same as those produced in the late 1930s. There were, however, some improvements, such as the adoption of larger brakes for both models and a larger dynamo for the Prefect, which was also now fitted with smaller

wheels. The Anglia was no longer available as a Standard or De Luxe, a single model combining features from both of the earlier cars was the only model available. Features such as the rear window blind, opening front screen and running boards of the previous De Luxe were no longer included. Initially, colours for both the Anglia and Prefect were limited to just Black or White. Pre 1940s cars had been available with Black, Blue and Grey paintwork. In 1949 the Anglia was

Ford Anglia.

Ford Prefect.

redesigned, with the original vertical front grille similar to that of the Prefect being replaced by a sloping style. The Prefect also received a restyled front, with the headlights now flush fitted into the front wings. There were also new colours available.

In 1953, both models were deleted

Ford Popular, and Popular instrument layout.

from the range, replaced by the new 100E models. The new 100E Anglia and Prefect were more expensive than the models they replaced, so Ford introduced a less well equipped and cheaper version of the original E series Anglia called the Popular. This was discontinued in 1959 when a new Popular based on the 100E Anglia was introduced

alongside the completely new 105E Anglia, with its unusual reverse sloping rear window.

11

Standard equipment for the Popular included a single windscreen wiper mounted above the windscreen, unlike the Anglia and Prefect models, which had two wipers fitted at the bottom of the windscreen. The Popular had no sun visor, and trafficators were an optional extra, though it did have an ammeter as well as a fuel gauge and speedometer, plus the Prefect engine.

NUMBERS PRODUCED FROM 1945 ONWARDS: Prefect 279,000, Anglia 159,000, Popular 155,000.
COLOURS (1949): Essex Blue, Channel Green, Bristol Fawn, Honey Beige, Black.
ENGINE: Four-cylinder, SV. Anglia bore 56.6mm, stroke 92.5mm, 933cc (56.93in^3), maximum bhp 23.4 at 4000rpm, Zenith carburettor. Prefect and Popular bore 63.5mm, stroke 92.5mm, 1172cc (71.52in^3) maximum bhp 30 at 4000rpm, Zenith carburettor.
GEARBOX: Three-speed, synchromesh on top and intermediate gears, floor-mounted gear change.
REAR AXLE: Spiral bevel, ratio 5.5:1.

BRAKES: Rod actuated, front and rear 10in drums.
STEERING: Worm and nut.
TYRES: Anglia and Popular 4.50 x 17, Prefect 5.00 x 16.
SUSPENSION: Transverse leaf springs front and rear with radius arms and hydraulic shock absorbers.
DIMENSIONS: Anglia **length** with overriders: 12ft 10in (3.911m); **width**: 4ft 9in (1.448m); **height**: 5ft 3in (1.6m); **wheelbase**: 7ft 6in (2.29m); **track**: front and rear 3ft 9in (1.143m); **ground clearance**: 8.87in (2.25cm); **turning circle**: 36ft (10.97m). Popular as Anglia except **length**: 12ft 7.5in (3.843m). Prefect as Anglia except **length** with overriders: 13ft 0.25in (3.968m); **height**: 5ft 3.5in (1.613m); **wheelbase**: 7ft 10in (2.388m); **ground clearance**: 8.75in (22.2cm).
APPROXIMATE WEIGHTS: Anglia 14cwt 2qtr 8lb (740kg), Popular 14cwt 2qtr (736kg), Prefect 15cwt 3qtr 1lb (805kg).
CAPACITIES: Fuel, Anglia 6.5 gallons (29.5 litres), Prefect 7 gallons (31.8 litres).

Note the addition of amber indicators on the front wings.

Ford Consul, Zephyr, Zodiac mark 1

Introduced at the 1950 Earls Court Motor Show with the slogan '5 Star Motoring,'

production of the Ford Consul and Zephyr Six commenced in early 1951 (the Zephyr name had already been used on a car in the USA). The Zephyr Zodiac, which was essentially a better-equipped Zephyr, was

All cars on this page are Consul models. The Black car is an early example with semaphore-type indicators, but has had amber indicators fitted below the bumpers at a later date.

not introduced until October 1953. It was around this time that convertible versions of the Consul and Zephyr began to appear. These had been developed by Carbodies of Coventry, perhaps better known for producing London Taxi Cabs. Estate cars, converted from saloon models by coachbuilder ED Abbott, appeared in late 1954.

Changes to the suspension, both front and rear, during the life of the cars were numerous. Other changes included revised gearbox ratios and clutch. Externally, the change from semaphore indicators to flashing units incorporated in the front and rear lights occurred in 1953, with the move to separate flashing rear indicators taking place in October 1955, just a few months before the cars were replaced by the mark 2 range in February 1956. Standard equipment for the Consul included ammeter, interior light, two sun

All cars (including instrument layout) on this page are Zephyr Six models.

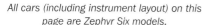

visors, two ashtrays, opening front quarter lights, bench-type front seat, and internal bonnet release. Additional equipment for the Zephyr Six included twin horns, overriders and larger tyres. The Zephyr Zodiac had a clock, cigar lighter, vanity mirror on the passenger sun visor, heater, windscreen washers, two-tone colour schemes for the body, internal door trim and leather seats, spot, fog and reversing lights, locking petrol cap, two wing mirrors, and gold-plated name scripts. Optional extras for the Consul and Zephyr Six included air-conditioning system, radio, and, for the Consul, overriders.

NUMBER PRODUCED: Consul 231,481, Zephyr Six 152,677, Zephyr Zodiac 22,634.
PRICE WHEN INTRODUCED: Consul £532, Zephyr Six £608. In 1953, following increases in purchase tax: Consul £666, Zephyr Six £754, Zephyr Zodiac £851, Consul convertible

Gear change diagram.

Blue and grey car is a Zephyr Zodiac: all others this page are Zephyr models.

15

£808, Zephyr Six convertible with power-operated hood £960.

COLOURS (1954): Black, Dorchester Grey, Canterbury Green, Lichfield Green, Winchester Blue, Westminster Blue, Bristol Fawn, and, for the Zephyr Zodiac only, Bristol Fawn, Canterbury Green and Winchester Blue, all with the upper body in Dorchester Grey.

ENGINE: Consul, four-cylinder, OHV, bore 79.37mm, stroke 76.2mm, 1508cc ($92in^3$), maximum bhp 47 at 4400rpm, Zenith carburettor. Zephyr Six, six-cylinder, OHV, bore 79.37mm, stroke 76.2mm, 2262cc ($138in^3$) maximum bhp 68 at 4200rpm, Zenith carburettor, Zephyr Zodiac as Zephyr Six except maximum bhp 71 at 4200rpm.

GEARBOX: Three-speed, synchromesh on top and intermediate gears, steering column gear change. Consul ratios at launch: top 4.625, 2nd 7.598, 1st 13.135; from February 1952, top 4.556, 2nd 7.704, 1st 14.898; from April 1953, top 4.556, 2nd 7.48, 1st 12.939, reverse 17.586. Zephyr Six ratios at

Three different styles of rear lights were fitted at various times.

The car on this page is a Zephyr Zodiac and has been fitted with non-standard amber rear indicators.

launch: top 4.375, 2nd 7.187, 1st 12.425; from February 1952, top 4.444, 2nd 7.514, 1st 14.531; from April 1953 top 4.444, 2nd 7.297, 1st 12.62, reverse 17.153. Note that the 1953 ratios also applied to Zephyr Zodiac.
REAR AXLE: Hypoid bevel, three-quarter floating, Consul ratio at launch 4.625:1, from February 1952 4.556:1. Zephyr Six as Consul except ratio at launch 4.375:1 from February 1952 4.444:1, Zephyr Zodiac 4.444:1.
BRAKES: Girling, hydraulic, front and rear 9in drums, handbrake under dashboard.
STEERING: Burman worm and peg.
TYRES: Consul 5.90 x 13, Zephyr Six and Zephyr Zodiac 6.40 x 13.
SUSPENSION: Front MacPherson coil springs and telescopic shock absorbers, rear semi-elliptic leaf springs and lever arm hydraulic shock absorbers.
DIMENSIONS: Consul **length:** 13ft 8.16in (4.17m); **width:** 5ft 3.98in (1.625m); **height:**

5ft 0.75in (1.543m); **wheelbase:** 8ft 4in (2.54m); **track:** front 4ft 2in (1.27m), rear 4ft 1in (1.245m); **ground clearance:** 6.5in (16.51cm); **turning circle:** 40ft 6in (12.34m), Zephyr Six and Zephyr Zodiac as Consul except **length:** 14ft 3.86in (4.365m); **wheelbase:** 8ft 8in (2.642m); **ground clearance:** 7in (17.78cm); **turning circle:** 41ft 6in (12.65m).
APPROXIMATE WEIGHTS: Consul 1 ton 3qtr 19lb (1603kg), Zephyr Six 1 ton 2cwt 3qtr 7lb (1159kg), Zephyr Zodiac 1ton 3cwt 3qtr (1207kg).
CAPACITIES: Fuel 9 gallons (40.914 litres).

Ford Consul, Zephyr, Zodiac mark 2

Introduced in February 1956 as 'The Three Graces,' the new cars had larger capacity engines, wider front brake shoes, and were longer, wider and taller than the models

The cars on this page are Consuls.

Instrument layout, Zephyr model.

they replaced, with the new Consul being as long as the previous Zephyr. The Zephyr Six was now called Zephyr and the Zephyr Zodiac became Zodiac. The initial range comprised Consul saloon and convertible, Zephyr saloon and convertible, and Zodiac saloon. Estate car conversions, again produced by ED Abbott, became available in October 1956, at the same time a Zodiac convertible was introduced, and there were

All cars on this page are early Zephyr models. Note the green car has a flat, not ribbed, rear panel.

Rear axle halfshafts were changed from
16- to 24-spline shafts in August 1956,
with further improvements of a mechanical
nature following during 1958. In February
1959 all models were redesigned with a
flatter roof-line. These became known as
the 'Low Line' models, and also featured a
new windscreen surround to take a deeper
windscreen, additional chrome-plated trim,
and revised rear lights. Interior changes
included safety padding for the fascia,
collapsible sun visors, door pull/armrests on
front and rear doors, locking front quarter
lights, twist release handbrake, and the gear
change was now enclosed in the steering
column shroud. Front disc brakes became
an option on all models in September 1960,
and then standard equipment in May 1961,
along with sealed beam headlights. Other
changes at this time included deleting some

*Front grille arrangements: top Consul, middle
Zephyr, bottom Zodiac. On left original cars; on
right 'Low Line models.'*

minor changes, with the Consul and Zephyr
featuring horizontally ribbed rear panels.
A Consul De Luxe saloon was introduced
in October 1957, and featured a two-tone
colour scheme and Zodiac-style interior, but
without a heater. The Zephyr received a new
front grille, and all models had redesigned
rear screen chrome trim, along with
changes to the steering and gear change.

Early Zodiac.

of the name badges from the rear bodywork. The mark 2 cars were discontinued in April 1962.

Standard equipment for the Consul included an ammeter, two sun visors, lockable glove box, bench-style front seat, opening quarter lights in the front doors, with the De Luxe adding duo-tone paint and chrome surrounds on side windows and rear lights, two-tone door trim, leather seats, front seat centre armrest, carpet instead of rubber floor covering, vanity mirror on passenger sun visor, cigar lighter, two coat hooks, two horns, and windscreen washers. Zodiac equipment generally as Consul De Luxe but also included a heater and whitewall tyres. For 1960 the Zephyr equipment included a temperature gauge instead of an ammeter, two-tone seats, carpet, bench-type front seat with centre armrest, armrests on all doors, and overriders. Optional extras for all models included a radio, and, for the Consul and Zephyr only, a heater. Borg Warner automatic transmission and overdrive became available as options in 1956, and, for the 1960 Zephyr, the options list included leather seats, rear seat centre armrest, front disc brakes and whitewall tyres.

NUMBER PRODUCED: Consul 350,244, Zephyr/Zodiac 301,417, of which approximately 80,000 were Zodiac models. These figures are for saloon and convertible models only. There were, in addition, approximately 5600 estate cars made.

PRICES WHEN INTRODUCED: Consul £781, Consul convertible £946, Zephyr £872, Zephyr convertible £1111, Zodiac £969. By 1962 the prices for the range had risen to Consul £844, Consul De Luxe £888, Consul convertible £1012, Zephyr £942, Zephyr estate £1182, Zodiac £1037, Zodiac convertible £1325, Zodiac estate £1285.

COLOURS (1956 all models): Black, Ivory, Wells Fawn, Sarum Blue, Carlisle Blue, Hereford Green, Warwick Green, Corfe Grey.

COLOURS (CONSUL DE LUXE): Body/roof colour, Kenilworth Blue/Black, Pembroke Coral/Dover White, Dover White/Ludlow Green, Ermine White/Linden Green, Cirrus White/Monza Red, Durham Beige/Pembroke Coral, Norwich Blue/Brecon Grey, Conway Yellow/

Black, Pompadour Blue/Black, Sunburst Yellow/Black, Shark Blue/Cirrus White, Imperial Maroon/Smoke Grey, Imperial Maroon/Chateau Grey, Black/Smoke Grey, Sapphire Blue/Pompadour Blue, Linden Green/Ermine White, Ambassador Blue/Pompadour Blue.

COLOURS (ZODIAC SALOON): Upper/lower body, Hereford Green/Ivory, Carlisle Blue/Wells Fawn, Ivory/Black, Corfe Grey/Norwich Blue, Smoke Grey/Pompadour Blue, Vulcan Grey/Smoke Grey, Windsor Grey/Ascot Grey, Newark Grey/Pembroke Coral, Pembroke Coral/Arundel Grey, Kenilworth Blue/Newark Grey, Ermine White/Ascot Grey, Ermine White/Pompadour Blue, Ermine White/Linden Green, Cirrus White/Lichen Green, Dover White/Ludlow Green, Black/Smoke Grey, Black/Norwich Blue, Black/Guildford Blue, Ludlow Green/Arundel Grey, Durham Beige/Newark Grey, Norwich Blue/Brecon Grey, Conway Yellow/Newark Grey, Sunburst Yellow/Cirrus White, Monza Red/Cirrus White, Imperial Maroon/Chateau Grey, Imperial Maroon/Smoke Grey, Shark Blue/Pompadour Blue, Ming Yellow/Ermine White, Ambassador Blue/Pompadour Blue, Lime Green /Regency Grey, Lime Green/Linden Green, Caribbean Turquoise/Ermine White, Rougement Red/Brecon Grey.

COLOURS (1960 ZEPHYR SALOON): Savoy Black, Ermine White, Pompadour Blue, Sapphire Blue, Ambassador Blue, Linden Green, Lime Green, Ming Yellow, Imperial Maroon, Regency Grey, Chateau Grey.

ENGINE: Consul, four-cylinder, OHV, bore 82.55mm, stroke 79.5mm, 1703cc (103.9in^3), maximum bhp 59 at 4400rpm, Zenith 34WIA carburettor. Zephyr and Zodiac, six-cylinder, OHV, bore 82.55mm, stroke 79.5mm, 2553cc (155.8in^3), maximum bhp 85 at 4400rpm, Zenith 36WIA carburettor.

GEARBOX: Three-speed, synchromesh on top and intermediate gears, column-mounted gear change. Ratios: Consul, top 4.11, 2nd 6.75, 1st 11.67, reverse 15.86; Zephyr and Zodiac top 3.90, 2nd 6.40, 1st 11.08, reverse 15.06. Optional Borg-Warner overdrive or automatic gearbox available for Zephyr and Zodiac only, automatic ratios, top 3.9, 2nd 5.596, 1st 8.981, reverse 15.67.

REAR AXLE: Hypoid bevel, three-quarter

All the cars on this and following pages are 'Low Line' models.

floating. Ratios: Consul 4.11:1; Zephyr and Zodiac 3.9:1 manual and automatic.

BRAKES: Girling hydraulic, front and rear 9in drums, then from 1961 servo assisted front 9.75in discs, rear 9in drums, handbrake mounted under dashboard.

STEERING: Initially worm and peg then from October 1957 recirculating ball.

TYRES: Consul 5.90 x 13, Zephyr and Zodiac saloons 6.40 x 13, estates 6.70 x 13.

SUSPENSION: Front MacPherson, coil springs

and hydraulic telescopic shock absorbers, rear semi-elliptic leaf springs and lever arm hydraulic shock absorbers.

DIMENSIONS (1956): Consul **length**: 14ft 4in (4.375m); **width**: 5ft 9in (1.753m); **height**: 5ft 2in (1.575m); **wheelbase**: 8ft 8.5in (2.654m); **track**: front 4ft 5in (1.346m), rear 4ft 4in (1.321m); **ground clearance**: 6.5in (16.5cm); **turning circle**: 35ft (10.7m). Zephyr and Zodiac as Consul except **wheelbase**: 8ft 11in (2.718m); **turning circle**: 36ft (10.97m). Zephyr **length**: 14ft 10.5in (4.539m). Zodiac **length**: 15ft 0.5in (4.585m).

DIMENSIONS (1959): As 1956 except **length**: Consul 14ft 5.75in (4.413m), Zephyr 14ft 11in (4.547m); **height**: all models 5ft 0.5in (1.537m).

APPROXIMATE WEIGHTS: Consul 1ton 2cwt 2qtr (1143kg); Zephyr 1ton 4cwt (1219kg), Zodiac 1ton 4cwt 2qtr (1244kg).

CAPACITIES: Fuel 10.5 gallons (47.67 litres). Boot saloon 18ft^3 (0.509m^3), estate 36ft^3 (1.019m^3) or 66ft^3 (1.868m^3) with rear seat folded down.

Rear light arrangements: top Consul, middle Zephyr, bottom Zodiac. Left original cars, on right 'Low Line models.'

Manual (left) and automatic gear change diagrams.

Zephyr model.

All cars on this page are Zodiac models.

Ford Anglia, Prefect, Popular, Squire, Escort 100E and Prefect 107E

Bearing some resemblance to the larger Ford models, the Consul and Zephyr, which had been introduced in 1950, the new Anglia and Prefect were introduced in October 1953 and December 1953 respectively. Then, in October 1955, De Luxe versions of both cars were introduced. These followed the introduction a month earlier of two estate car models: the Squire, and the less well-equipped Escort. In appearance the estates looked like vans, but they had split upper and lower tailgates instead of opening doors.

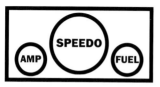

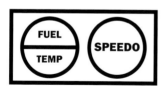

Instrument layouts: Anglia (above), and Anglia De Luxe.

Changes during the life of the 100E range included the driver's seat of the Anglia incorporating a tipping mechanism, like that of the front passenger seat, to make access to the rear seats easier, the adoption of a passenger sun visor, larger brakes fitted to all models, changes to gearbox ratios, and, for the Prefect, wind-up instead of pull-up rear windows. There were also styling changes, with three different types of rear lights, new instrument panels and bumpers, repositioned

Anglia models. Note that the car at the top is fitted with an early-style front grille.

rear badges, and an enlarged rear window. The Anglia also had a change of front grille in 1957, with the original three-bar design being replaced by a simpler, mesh-style item. Standard equipment for the Anglia originally included an ammeter, single ashtray, driver's sun visor, separate bucket-style front seats, opening front quarter lights, and a single horn. The Anglia De Luxe, in addition to the above, featured two rear ashtrays, passenger sun visor, two horns, chrome window surrounds and bodyside strip, and two wing mirrors. Prefect equipment generally followed that of the Anglia models.

Both De Luxe models eventually lost their wing mirrors, but gained a lockable glove box. Optional equipment included a heater, radio, and, for a short while, a form of automatic transmission.

By the end of 1959 production of the Anglia had ceased, but a new model, the Popular, based on the Anglia and available in both basic and De Luxe forms was introduced; then discontinued in May 1962. The Prefect model was available from August 1959 until March 1961, with the new 997cc OHV engine and four-speed gearbox as fitted to the Anglia 105E. These revised Prefects can usually be identified by the additional small piece of chrome strip on the front wings, creating what is often referred to as a 'dogleg' pattern.

Prefect models. The upper car is an early model with circular rear reflectors.

NUMBER PRODUCED: Anglia 345,841, Prefect 100E 255,655, Squire 17,812, Escort 33,131, Popular 126,115, Prefect 107E 38,154.

PRICE WHEN INTRODUCED: Anglia £360, Prefect £395, in 1955 a De Luxe Anglia was £542 and a Prefect £596.

COLOURS (1953): Black, Bristol Fawn,

Dorchester Grey, Lichfield Green, Edinburgh Green (Prefect only).

COLOURS (1957): Black, Ambassador Blue, Carlisle Blue, Bristol Fawn, Corfe Grey, Hereford Green, and, for Anglia, Escort and Squire only, Dover White, Durham Beige, Kenilworth Blue. Anglia and Prefect only Guildford Blue, Ivory.

COLOURS (1959): Two-tone schemes for the Prefect 107E (lower body colour first) included, Imperial Maroon/Smoke Grey, Shark Blue/Pompadour Blue, Sunburst Yellow/Cirrus White, Vulcan Grey/Smoke Grey.

ENGINE: Four-cylinder SV, bore 63.5mm, stroke 92.5mm, 1172cc (71.52in^3), maximum bhp 36 at 4400rpm, Solex 26ZIC carburettor.

GEARBOX (1955): Three-speed, synchromesh on top and intermediate gears, floor-mounted gear change, ratios top 4.429, 2nd 8.25, 1st 15.07, reverse 19.71.

GEARBOX (from August 1955): as above except ratios 2nd 8.89, 1st 16.23, reverse 21.22.

Gear change diagram for three-speed gearbox.

The car in the top two photos is a Popular Basic model: note lack of side trim and no inserts in screen rubbers. The lower two cars are Popular De Luxe models.

GEARBOX (from May 1957): as August 1955 except 1st 17.24.

REAR AXLE: Spiral bevel three-quarter floating, ratio all years 4.429:1.

Prefect 107E details below.

ENGINE: Four-cylinder OHV, bore 80.96mm, stroke 48.41mm, 997cc (60.84in³), maximum bhp 39 at 5000rpm, Solex 30ZIC-2 carburettor.

GEARBOX: Four-speed, synchromesh on top three gears, floor-mounted gear change. Ratios: top 4.429, 3rd 6.254, 2nd 10.612, 1st 18.239, reverse 23.934.

REAR AXLE: Spiral bevel, three-quarter floating. Ratio 4.429:1.

BRAKES: Hydraulic, front and rear 7in drums until January 1955 then 8in drums. Floor-mounted handbrake.

STEERING: Worm and peg.

TYRES: 5.20 x 13.

SUSPENSION: Front independent coil springs with double-acting shock absorbers and stabilizer bar, rear semi-elliptic leaf springs and telescopic shock absorbers.

DIMENSIONS: **Length**: 12ft 5.75in (3.842m); **width**: 5ft 0.75in (1.54m); **height**: 4ft 10.75in (1.467m); **wheelbase**: 7ft 3in (2.209m); **track**: front 4ft 0in (1.219m), rear 3ft 11.25in (1.207m); **ground clearance**: 7in (17.8cm); **turning circle**: 32ft 9in (9.982m). Squire/Escort **length**: 11ft 9.75in (3.6m); **width**: 5ft 0.75in (1.54m); **height**: 5ft 2.75in (1.594m).

APPROXIMATE WEIGHTS: Anglia/Popular 15cwt 10lb (766.6kg), Prefect 15cwt 3qtr 24lb (811.1kg).

CAPACITIES: Fuel 7 gallons (31.82 litres). Boot saloons 10ft³ (0.283m³), estates 13.5ft³ (0.382m³) or 41.5ft³ (1.174m³) with rear seat folded down.

The green car is a Prefect 107E; the blue one is an Escort.

Gear change diagram for a four-speed gearbox.

Ford Anglia 105E and 123E

Introduced in September 1959, the new Anglia now featured tail fins, which were becoming popular in the USA. This style of rear wing was also included on the Triumph Herald also launched at the 1959 Motor Show. However, whereas the square rear window of the Herald sloped outwards, as was the normal convention, the Anglia's rear window sloped inwards, creating a car that looked like nothing seen on British roads until the Ford Consul Classic arrived in 1961. The theory behind this style of rear window was that it would increase headroom for rear seat passengers. Initially introduced as Basic and De Luxe saloon models with 997cc engines, an estate model in both Basic and De Luxe form appeared in 1961, and, in October 1962, the Anglia Super, with an 1198cc engine and all-synchromesh gearbox from the Ford Cortina, was introduced. The Super model had more equipment than the De Luxe, it had larger brakes, and was immediately identifiable by its contrastingly-coloured side flash and roof. The 1198 engine became available as an option for the De Luxe models. Basic models could be identified by their smaller, non full-width front grille, a style also adopted for the van variants (introduced in 1961, initially called the Thames van, and available as either 5cwt or 7cwt models).

All cars this page are early models with combined white sidelight and indicator lenses. Note that some cars were fitted with whitewall tyres.

Changes during the life of the Anglia included the adoption of separate front sidelights and indicators, and a Ford carburettor replacing the Solex unit. Standard equipment for the De Luxe model, in addition to the Basic, included a temperature gauge, passenger sun visor, door armrests, lockable glove box, two rear ashtrays, two-tone seats and door trim, opening rear quarter windows, and bright metal

interior and exterior trim. Optional extras for both models included a heater and radio, and, for the De Luxe, leather upholstery, two-tone paint scheme featuring a different roof colour, whitewall tyres, and the 1198cc engine with all-synchromesh gearbox. The Super models had larger brakes. Super standard equipment, in addition to De Luxe, included a heater, windscreen washers, cigarette lighter, padded fascia top, carpet instead of rubber floor covering, grab handles for rear seat passengers (this at a time when seatbelts were not fitted). Seatbelt anchorage points for front seat passengers were fitted from 1964, ahead of the Government's requirement that all cars from 1965 on had to have front seatbelts.

NUMBER PRODUCED: Basic 122,242, De Luxe 752,967, Super 79,223, Base estate 6686, De Luxe estate 122,842.
PRICE WHEN INTRODUCED: Basic £589, De Luxe £610.
COLOURS (1962): Basic model, Ascot Grey, Ermine White, Aqua Blue, Ambassador Blue, Lime Green. De Luxe in addition to above Savoy Black, Windsor Grey, Imperial Maroon. Two-tone schemes upper colour first Ermine White/Ascot Grey, Ermine White/Lime Green, Ermine White/Aqua Blue, Ascot Grey/Windsor Grey, Ascot Grey/Imperial Maroon, Ascot Grey/ Ambassador Blue.
COLOURS (1967) included: Ermine White, Purbeck Grey, Lagoon, Anchor Blue, Seafoam Blue, Spruce Green and in addition for Super models only Blue Mink, Venetian Gold.

ENGINE (997): Four-cylinder, OHV, bore 80.96mm, stroke 48.4mm, 997cc (60.84in^3), maximum bhp 39 at 5000rpm, Solex 30ZIC-2 then Solex 30PSEI carburettor until 1966 when a Ford unit was fitted.

Base model fitted with De Luxe front grille.

Dashboard diagram.

This car is an early Super model.

The car above has separate sidelights and indicators. The other cars on this page are final versions with sidelights incorporated in headlights, and separate amber front indicators.

GEARBOX: Four-speed, synchromesh on top three gears, floor-mounted gear change. Ratios top 4.125, 3rd 5.826, 2nd 9.884, 1st 16.987, reverse 22.292.
REAR AXLE: Hypoid bevel, semi-floating, ratio 4.125:1.
ENGINE (1200): Four-cylinder, OHV, bore 80.96mm, stroke 58.17mm, 1198cc ($73.11in^3$), maximum bhp 53 at 4800rpm, Solex B30PSEI carburettor.

GEARBOX: Four-speed, all-synchromesh, floor-mounted gearlever. Ratios: top 4.12, 3rd 5.925, 2nd 9.885, 1st 14.625, reverse 16.347.
REAR AXLE: Hypoid bevel, semi-floating. Ratio: 4.125:1.
BRAKES: Girling, front and rear 8in drums, floor-mounted handbrake (note Super had wider brake drums, front 1.75in, rear 1.5in).
STEERING: Burman recirculating ball.
TYRES: 5.20 x 13 saloons, spare wheel stored vertically in boot against rear seat, 5.60 x 13 estate, spare wheel under flap in boot floor.
SUSPENSION: Front MacPherson coil spring

Gear change diagram.

30

*Anglia estates feature a different roof
colour, but no side flash.*

and double acting shock absorbers with anti-roll bar, rear semi-elliptic leaf springs and double acting lever arm shock absorbers.
DIMENSIONS: **Length**: 12ft 9.5in (3.898m), or 12ft 11.75in (3.905m) with overriders; **width**: 4ft 9.5in (1.46m); **height**: 4ft 8.5in (1.435m); **wheelbase**: 7ft 6.5in (2.292m); **track**: front 3ft 10.25in (1.175m), rear 3ft 9.75in (1.162m); **ground clearance**: 6in (15.2cm); **turning circle**: 32.4ft (9.9m).

Estate as above except **length**: 12ft 10.25in (3.92m); **height**: 4ft 7.5in (1.4097m).
APPROXIMATE WEIGHTS: De Luxe 14cwt 2qtr (737kg), Super 14cwt 3qtr (750kg), estate 15cwt 3qtr (801kg).
CAPACITIES: Fuel 7 gallons (31.8 litres). Boot saloon 11.5ft^3 (0.618m^3), estate 15.25ft^3 (0.811m^3) or 35.5ft^3 (1.889m^3) with rear seat folded down.

The smaller front grille on the van is the same as that fitted to Basic saloon models, but the rear styling differed between vans and estates.

Ford Consul Classic and Capri

The Consul Classic was introduced in April 1961, and the Capri in July 1961. Both were discontinued in September 1963, though a special version of the Capri, a GT model, was launched in February 1963 and then discontinued in July 1964. This idea of introducing special editions at the end of the intended life of its models was common practice with the Ford Motor Company. The Classic was originally intended to fill the gap between the smaller Ford Anglia and the larger Consul/Zephyr models ahead of the introduction of the Cortina in 1962, which was initially called the Consul Cortina. However, the Classic's ultimate successor was the Corsair. Both the Consul Classic and Capri models were initially fitted with a 1340cc engine. However, a little over a year later this engine was replaced by a 1500cc unit, which came with an all-synchromesh gearbox. Both engines were derivations of the Anglia 105E engine: the increase in engine size being achieved by increasing the stroke. Also taken from the Anglia was the style of rear window for the Classic. Completely new, though, were four headlights.

The initial range comprised Classic and

All cars on this page are Capri models.

Classic De Luxe, both available as a two- or four-door saloon, and a Capri two-door coupé. The early cars with 1340 engines were known as 109E models, and the 1500-engined cars 116E models. Equipment for the standard Classic 116E model included temperature gauge, variable instrument lighting, driver's sun visor, split front bench seat, variable speed wipers (rheostat controlled), opening front quarter lights, and, on the two-door models, opening rear quarter lights, and a single horn. De Luxe model added windscreen washers, headlight flasher, passenger sun visor, lockable glove box, front parcel shelf, cigarette lighter, rear ashtray, carpet floor covering, padded door armrests incorporating door handles,

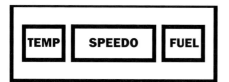

Instrument layout.

All cars on this page are Capri models. The black car is a GT.

two coat hooks, two-tone door and seat trim, two-tone paint scheme, front-door-operated courtesy light, twin horns, bright metal trim with five stars on the radiator grille, and a decorative panel between the boot lid and rear bumper. Optional extras included heater, whitewall tyres and steering column gear change for both models, and, for the De Luxe, leather or vinyl upholstery. Radios, wing mirrors, etc, were dealer-fitted accessories.

Standard equipment for the Capri 109E model included a temperature gauge, variable instrument lighting, driver and passenger sun visors, lockable glove box, full-width front

All green cars on this page and overleaf are Classics.

parcel shelf, cigarette lighter, bucket-type front seats and occasional rear seat, variable speed wipers, windscreen washers, headlight flasher, opening front quarter lights and wind-down rear quarter windows, two-tone door and seat trim, armrests incorporating door handles, carpeted floor, door-operated courtesy light, twin horns, choice of single or two-tone paint scheme. Optional extras included heater, whitewall tyres, steering column gear change, leather or vinyl upholstery.

NUMBER PRODUCED: Classic 109E 84,694, Capri 109E 11,143, Classic 116E 26,531, Capri 116E 7573, Capri GT 2002.
PRICE WHEN INTRODUCED: Classic standard two-door £745, standard four-door and De Luxe two-door £773, De Luxe four-door £802, Capri £916.
COLOURS (1962): Classic, standard and De Luxe, single tone, Savoy Black, Ermine White, Ascot Grey, Windsor Grey, Ambassador Blue, Aqua Blue, Lime Green, Goodwood Green, Panama Yellow, Imperial Maroon, and for De Luxe only, two-tone upper body first, Ascot Grey/Ambassador Blue, Ascot Grey/Windsor Grey, Ascot Grey/Imperial Maroon, Ermine White/Ascot Grey, Ermine White/Aqua Blue, Ermine White/Lime Green.
ENGINE (1340): Four-cylinder, OHV, bore 80.96mm, stroke 65.07mm, 1340cc (81.77in³), maximum bhp 56.5 at 5200rpm, Zenith 32VN carburettor.

GEARBOX: Four-speed, synchromesh on top three gears, floor-mounted gear change, with optional steering column change. Ratios: top 4.125, 3rd 5.826, 2nd 9.884, 1st 16.987, reverse 22.292.
REAR AXLE: Hypoid bevel, semi-floating. Ratio: 4.125:1.
ENGINE (1500): Four-cylinder, OHV, bore 80.97mm, stroke 72.8mm, 1498cc (91.5in³) maximum bhp 64 at 4600rpm, Zenith 33VN-2 carburettor. GT model, maximum bhp 78 at 5200rpm, Weber 28/36 DCD carburettor.
GEARBOX: Four-speed, all-synchromesh, floor-mounted gear change with optional steering column change. Ratios: top 4.125, 3rd 5.826, 2nd 9.884, 1st 14.245, reverse 16.347.
REAR AXLE: Hypoid bevel, semi-floating. Ratio: 4.125:1.
BRAKES: Girling, front 9.5in discs, rear 9in drums. Handbrake mounted under dashboard.
STEERING: Burman, recirculating ball.
TYRES: 5.60 x 13.
SUSPENSION: Front, independent with coil springs, double acting hydraulic telescopic shock absorbers and anti-roll bar, rear semi-elliptic leaf springs with hydraulic double acting lever type shock absorbers.
DIMENSIONS: Classic, **length**: 14ft 2.75in (4.337m); **width**: 5ft 5.25in (1.657m); **height**: 4ft 6.5in (1.384m); **wheelbase**: 8ft 3in (2.514m); **track**: front and rear 4ft 1.5in (1.257m); **ground clearance**: 6.5in (16.5cm); **turning circle**: 34ft (10.36m). Capri as

Classic except **height** :4ft 4.5in (1.333m).
APPROXIMATE WEIGHTS: Classic two-door and Capri 18cwt 2qtr (940kg).
CAPACITIES: Fuel 9 gallons (41 litres). Boot 21ft^3 (0.594m^3).

Ford Consul Corsair

The four-door De Luxe was first produced in June 1963, with other models following from July through to September. With the official introduction taking place at the Earls Court motor show in October 1963, it was the first Ford to be produced at the new factory in Halewood, near Liverpool in Merseyside. The Consul Corsair, which bore a strong resemblance to the Ford USA Thunderbird of the same period, replaced the Consul Classic, and inherited its 1498cc engine. The body, however, was built on a lengthened Cortina floorpan, and much of the internal structure, such as the scuttle, bulkhead, inner engine bay panels and door shells also came from the Cortina. The Corsair outer door skins, though, were totally different to the Classic and Cortina, having no hint of a swage and featuring flush-fitting door handles.

An advantage over the Cortina was the lengthened floorpan, which provided a three-inch longer wheelbase, and thus increased legroom for rear seat passengers (there was no increase in boot space, though). The double skinning over the central transmission tunnel and fibreglass-lined bulkhead were claimed to reduce noise.

Other innovations included 'lube for life' greaseless points, and a printed circuit board with plug-in feature behind the fascia replaced conventional wiring. The initial range included two- and four-door Standard, De Luxe and GT models, with an automatic option following in December 1963. It should be noted that Ford brochures use De Luxe, de Luxe and de luxe to describe the higher specification model. Standard equipment included temperature gauge, variable speed windscreen wipers (rheostat controlled), steering column-mounted light switch, headlight dipswitch and indicators with push button on end of the stalk for horn (headlight flasher on De Luxe), front bench seat for four-door models, split bench-type seat for two-door models, driver's sun visor, ashtray in centre of dashboard, interior light, combined armrests and door pulls, glove box, rubber floor covering, opening front quarter lights. De Luxe added windscreen washers, coat hooks, door-operated courtesy

Corsair De Luxe automatic.

light, passenger sun visor, two rear ashtrays, horn ring, two-tone horn, full-width front parcel shelf, carpets instead of rubber floor covering, aluminium kick plates on the bottoms of doors. GT model featured power-assisted brakes, revolution counter (tachometer), ammeter, oil pressure gauge, armrest/glove box, separate front bucket seats, floor-mounted gear change and more. Optional extras included heater (standard equipment on all models from 1965), whitewall tyres, automatic transmission, and, for Standard and De Luxe models, floor-mounted gear change with separate front bucket seats. Two-tone paint was available for De Luxe and GT. Dealer-fitted options included radio, wing mirrors, front fog and long-range driving lights, reversing light, special wheel trims, roof rack, seatbelts and more. There were changes to the interior a year after the car's introduction, with the light switch moved from the steering column to the dashboard and a new multipurpose lighting stalk on the steering column, together with safety features, such as a revised deep-dish steering wheel, one-piece dashboard crash padding, and the quartic shaped horn ring on the De Luxe and GT was replaced by a three-quarter piece item to make it easier to see the instrument panel.

NUMBER PRODUCED: Standard two-door

335, four-door 953, De Luxe two-door 33,352, four-door 103,094, GT two-door 6610, four-door 15,247.

PRICE WHEN INTRODUCED: Standard two-door £653, four-door and De Luxe two-door £677, GT four-door £840. Optional extra prices included heater £15, automatic transmission £82, bucket seats and floor gear change for De Luxe £12, two-tone paint scheme £6, and whitewall tyres £7.

COLOURS: Ermine White, Platinum Grey,

FUEL	SPEEDO	TEMP

Instrument layout Standard and De Luxe.

The top photo is of a Corsair GT, whilst the photo above is of a De Luxe.

Early cars can be identified by the Corsair badge on the nose.

OIL	AMP	FUEL	SPEEDO	TEMP

REVS

Above: instrument layout GT model. Note that the revolution counter was mounted below the dashboard.

Windsor Grey, Ambassador Blue, Aqua Blue, Light Blue, Spruce Green, Goodwood Green, Tuscan Yellow, Imperial Maroon, Monaco Red. Two-tones, main body colour first: Platinum Grey/Ermine White, Aqua Blue/Ermine White, Spruce Green/Ermine White, Ambassador Blue/Platinum Grey, Imperial Maroon/Platinum Grey.

ENGINE: Four-cylinder, OHV, bore 80.97mm, stroke 72.8mm, 1498cc (91.4in^3), maximum bhp 59.5 at 4600rpm, Zenith 33VN-2 carburettor. GT as above except maximum bhp 79 at 5200rpm, Weber 28/36 DCD22 carburettor.

GEARBOX: Four-speed, all-synchromesh, steering column or floor-mounted gear change. Ratios: top 3.90, 3rd 5.507, 2nd 9.344, 1st 13.818, reverse 15.456. GT: top 3.90, 3rd 5.471, 2nd 9.340, 1st 13.845, reverse 15.483. Borg-Warner automatic transmission optional.

REAR AXLE: Hypoid bevel, semi-floating. Ratio: all models 3.90:1.

BRAKES: Girling, front 9.5in discs, rear 9in drums, power-assisted on GT model, handbrake under dashboard.

STEERING: Burman recirculatory ball.

TYRES: 5.60 x 13.

SUSPENSION: Front MacPherson strut-type, independent coil springs, Armstrong shock absorbers and anti-roll bar, rear semi-elliptic leaf springs with Armstrong double acting

De Luxe (name badge is deluxe but brochure is De Luxe).

telescopic shock absorbers. Note suspension was based on the Cortina GT system.
DIMENSIONS: Length: 14ft 8.75in (4.49m); **width:** 5ft 3.5in (1.613m); **height:** 4ft 9.25in (1.454m); **wheelbase:** 8ft 5in (2.565m); **track:** front 4ft 2in (1.27m), rear 4ft 1.6in (1.26m); **ground clearance:** 6.75in (17cm); **turning circle:** 36ft (10.97m).
APPROXIMATE WEIGHTS: Standard two-door 17cwt 2qtr 2lb (890kg), De Luxe two-door 17cwt 2qtr 15lb (896kg), four-door 17cwt 3qtr 19lb (911kg).
CAPACITIES: Fuel 8 gallons (36.4litres). Boot 20.9ft³ (0.591m³).

Floor gear change diagram.

This blue and white car is a De Luxe. The convertible, a Crayford conversion.

Ford Corsair V4

Introduced in September 1965 with the slogan 'We've got a V in our bonnet,' the Corsair now featured completely new engines of a V formation. These engines were also used in the Zephyr range but

never in the Cortina. A Corsair GT estate was launched at the 1966 Geneva motor show, once again the conversion from saloon to estate was carried out by Abbots. Also available was a Corsair convertible produced by Crayford Engineering, the company responsible for many convertibles in the

All cars on this page are GT models. The car above has a roof rack typical of the era.

1960s, including the Wolseley Hornets given away in a competition organised by Heinz Foods.

In January 1967, a Corsair 2000E, available only as a four-door saloon, was introduced, and ultimately replaced the GT saloon model (though the 2000E and GT existed side-by-side for a few months). The Corsair estate was discontinued in February 1968, and the saloons were discontinued in June 1970. Changes from the Consul Corsair included dropping the Consul name,

V4 engine cars have V-shaped trim on the nose, and Aeroflow vents in the rear quarter panels.

A Corsair 2000E.

revisions to the badging, the introduction of the two new engines of 1662cc and 1996cc replacing the single 1498cc engine, and the new Aeroflow heating and ventilation system. This featured fresh air vents at either end of the dashboard and extractor vents in the rear pillars that then pulled the stale air out of the car as it was driven along. It also pulled warm air from the heater at the front to the rear seat passengers who then benefited from this increased flow. Other changes included revisions to the steering column gear change and clutch, lighter steering, new dashboard with instruments of a circular design, restyled seats, larger front disc brakes, self adjusting

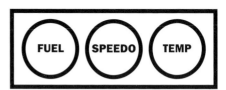

De Luxe instrument layout.

rear brakes, and an increased fuel tank capacity from eight gallons to ten.

The range at launch included De Luxe and GT four-door saloons with manual or automatic transmission. The De Luxe had the 1662 engine and the GT the 1996. The Standard model was deleted and two-door models were for export markets only. The range ultimately became De Luxe 1700 and 2000 saloons, 2000 estate and 2000E saloon. Standard equipment for De Luxe included temperature gauge, heating and ventilation system with two-speed fan, padding to the top and bottom of the fascia and the edge of the full-width front parcel shelf, glove box, two sun visors, two-speed windscreen wipers, windscreen washers, three ashtrays, interior courtesy light, combined door pulls and armrests, bench front seat, carpet floor covering, and coat hooks. GT added ammeter, oil pressure gauge, tachometer (revolution counter), courtesy light operated by front doors, cigarette lighter, bucket-style front seats, centre console with glove box, armrest and ashtray. 2000E generally as GT without the side trim but added clock, radio, reclining front bucket seats, vinyl-covered roof, special wheel trims, reversing lights, overriders, carpeted boot with spare wheel cover incorporating tool bag, boot and under bonnet lights. Optional extras on the early models included a two-tone

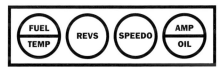

Instrument layout GT.

The cars on this page are Crayford convertible versions of the Corsair.

paint scheme, whitewall tyres, automatic transmission, and optional for the De Luxe was floor gear change and bucket seats. Later cars had inertia reel seatbelts, metallic paint and automatic transmission, whilst the De Luxe had floor gear change with a choice of fixed or reclining front seats, radio, and wide rim wheels with radial tyres.

NUMBER PRODUCED: De Luxe two-door 6450, four-door 118,065, GT two-door 1534, four-door 31,566, estate car 940.

PRICES WHEN INTRODUCED: De Luxe £785, GT £909. In July 1966, De Luxe £803, GT £928, GT estate £1149.

COLOURS (1967): Saloon and estate, Ermine White, Purbeck Grey, Alpine Green, Lagoon Blue, Saloons Only, Anchor Blue, Dragoon Red and metallics, Blue Mink, Saluki Bronze, Silver Fox.

ENGINE (1965): All four-cylinder V configuration, OHV. De Luxe, bore 93.66mm, stroke 60.35mm, 1662cc (101.4in^3), maximum bhp 81.5 at 4750rpm, Zenith 36IV carburettor. GT bore 93.66mm, stroke 72.41mm, 1996cc (121.8in^3), maximum bhp 93.0 at 4750rpm, Zenith 36IV carburettor.

GEARBOX: Four-speed, all-synchromesh, steering column change on De Luxe, floor-mounted on GT. Ratios: De Luxe top 3.78, 3rd 5.333, 2nd 9.05, 1st 13.382, reverse 14.968; GT top 3.78, 3rd 5.287, 2nd 7.592, 1st 11.217, reverse 12.539.

REAR AXLE: Hypoid bevel, semi-floating. Ratio: all models 3.777:1.

ENGINE (1969): As 1965 models except De Luxe 1700 maximum bhp 84 at 4750rpm, Ford carburettor. De Luxe 2000 and 2000E, maximum bhp 102.0 at 5000rpm, Weber DIF4 carburettor.

GEARBOX: Four-speed, all-synchromesh, steering column gear change on De Luxe, floor-mounted on 2000E. De Luxe 1700 ratios: top 3.78, 3rd 5.299, 2nd 7.985, 1st 12.245, reverse 13.869. All 2000 models ratios: top 3.78, 3rd 5.276, 2nd 7.592, 1st 11.225, reverse 12.555.

REAR AXLE: Hypoid bevel, semi-floating. Ratio: all models 3.777:1.

BRAKES: Front 9.625in discs, rear 9in drums, power-assisted on 2000 models.

STEERING: Burman recirculatory ball.

TYRES: De Luxe and GT 5.60 x 13, De Luxe 2000 and 2000E 165 x 13.

SUSPENSION: Front, MacPherson strut-type, independent coil springs and telescopic shock absorbers and anti-roll bar, rear semi-elliptic leaf springs with telescopic shock absorbers. GT model with rear axle locating links.

DIMENSIONS: Length: 14ft 8.75in (4.49m); **width:** 5ft 3.5in (1.613m); **height:** 4ft 7.5in (1.41m), **wheelbase:** 8ft 5in (2.565m); **track:**

GT models can be identified by a small badge on rear wing.

GT estate with non-factory-fitted fabric sunroof.

front 4ft 2in (1.27m), rear 4ft 1.6in (1.26m); **ground clearance**: 6.75in (17cm); **turning circle**: 36ft 7in (11.2m).
APPROXIMATE WEIGHTS: GT saloon 19cwt 1qtr 10lb (982kg), GT estate 1ton 1cwt (1070kg), 2000E 1ton 12lb (1023kg).
CAPACITIES: Fuel 10 gallons (45.5 litres), boot saloon 20.9ft³ (0.595m³), estate 29.3ft³ (0.83m³), or 59.9ft³ (1.70m³) with rear seat folded down.

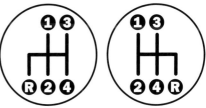

Left, original floor gear change. Right, gear change from 1967.

Ford Cortina mark 1

Introduced in September 1962, the Cortina had been given the codename 'Archbishop,' in an attempt to upstage the German Ford Taunus (codename Cardinal). However, this name had been given to the Taunus by Ford USA who, having already named another of its cars the Falcon, decided to use another American bird's name: the Cardinal. The Cortina name came from the Italian resort that had previously been used for the Winter Olympic games, but, like the Ford Capri and Classic that had appeared earlier, the original intention was to use the Consul name, with the 1200 engine model being known as the Consul 225, and the 1500 engine model the Consul 255, but, at the last minute, the car appeared as the Consul Cortina.

The Consul name was dropped in 1964 when the car received styling changes to the front grille and lights, though the unique rear lights remained unchanged. Other styling changes were deletion of the Di-Noc imitation wood on the sides of the Super estate, and the introduction of a new dashboard incorporating swivelling vents for the new Aeroflow ventilation. This was the second change to the dashboard since

De Luxe.

the car's launch, with the original strip-type speedometer being replaced by a circular version in September 1963.

The Cortina was the first Ford to be

An early Lotus Cortina.

fitted with Aeroflow ventilation that enabled the occupants to have fresh air to the face while the rear extractor vents in the rear quarter panels drew stale air out of the car and also pulled the warm air from heater, which now became a standard item instead of optional equipment, into the rear passenger compartment. This system would ultimately lead to the loss of the opening front quarter lights.

Mechanical changes at the same time included the adoption of front disc brakes for all models, and trailing radius arms being added to the rear suspension of the GT model. The Lotus Cortina retained its A-frame coil spring suspension until June 1965 when it then adopted the GT suspension of leaf springs and trailing arms. Earlier changes had been the introduction of 'Lube for life' chassis and childproof locks in 1963, and later changes included bucket-type front seats, with floor-mounted gear change becoming the standard fitting across the range. Steering column gear change and bench seats were available as options on some models from October 1965. The range at launch included Standard, De Luxe and Super two- and four-door saloons

This car has the two-tone paint scheme, bright metal side trim and wheel trims usually associated with the Super models.

(the Lotus Cortina, available only as a two-door saloon, followed in January 1963). In March 1963, the De Luxe and Super estates and GT saloon appeared. It should be noted that, although brochures used the spelling 'De Luxe,' the badges on the cars appeared as 'deluxe.' All models were replaced by the Cortina mark 2 in October 1966.

It was usual to introduce any significant changes and new models at the London Motor Show, held at Earls Court in October each year. Standard equipment for the Consul Cortina De Luxe included temperature gauge, headlight flasher, individual front bucket seats with floor-mounted gear change, combined armrest and door pulls, opening front quarter lights on four-door models, with opening rear quarter lights on two-door models, driver and

passenger sun visors (driver's only on Standard model), glove box with lid, padded fascia, and door scuff plates. Super added heater, windscreen washers, colour-keyed carpet instead of rubber floor covering, cigarette lighter, wheel trim rings, bright metal exterior trim and two-tone colour scheme. The front seat was of the bench-type with steering column gear change. Note that the two-tone paint finish of the original De Luxe estate, featuring a different coloured roof and side flash, was applied to the Super estate when it lost its imitation wood side trim, and the De Luxe then lost its two-tone paint scheme. Optional equipment included whitewall tyres and, for De Luxe, 1500cc engine (automatic transmission was available for all models with 1500cc engine).

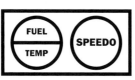

Early instrument layout.

Later instrument layout.

Below: Super estate with its imitation wood side trim reminiscent of American 'Woodies' station wagons. Later Super estates had a more subdued appearance.

NUMBER PRODUCED: Standard saloon 34,514, De Luxe saloon 704,871, Super saloon 77,753, GT 76,947, Lotus Cortina 3301, De Luxe estate 108,219 Super estate 7786.

PRICE WHEN INTRODUCED: Standard two-door £639, De Luxe four-door £687, note a reduction in Purchase Tax in November 1962 brought the prices of the cars down so that in 1963, following the introduction of Super and GT models, the prices were Standard two-door £573, De Luxe four-door £616, Super four-door £688, GT two-door £749, four-door £767.

COLOURS: Ermine White, Windsor Grey, Ambassador Blue, Light Blue, Goodwood Green, Monaco Red, Imperial Maroon and more.

ENGINE: Four-cylinder, OHV, Standard and De Luxe, bore 80.97mm, stroke 58.17mm, 1198cc (73.11in^3), maximum bhp 54 at 5000rpm, Solex B3PSE1-2 carburettor. Super (optional for De Luxe), bore 80.97mm, stroke 72.8mm, 1498cc (91.5in^3), maximum bhp 65 at 4800rpm, Zenith 33VN2 carburettor. GT as Super except, maximum bhp 78 at 5200rpm, Weber 28/36 carburettor. Lotus Cortina, four-cylinder, DOHC, bore 82.5mm, stroke

72.746mm, 1558cc (95.07in^3) maximum bhp 105 at 5500rpm, two Weber 40DCOE2 carburettors.

GEARBOX: Four-speed, all-synchromesh, floor- or steering column-mounted gear change dependent on model. 1200 saloon ratios: top 4.125, 3rd 5.825, 2nd 9.884, 1st 14.615, reverse 16.347; 1200 estate ratios: top 4.444, 3rd 6.275, 2nd 10.648, 1st 15.745, reverse 17.612; 1500 saloon and estate ratios: top 3.90, 3rd 5.507, 2nd 9.344,

This car, and those on the following pages, are later models with revised front grille and Aeroflow ventilation.

1st 13.818, reverse 15.456. Automatic: top 3.90, 2nd 5.66, 1st 9.32, reverse 8.15. Lotus Cortina ratios: top 3.9, 3rd 4.797, 2nd 6.396, 1st 9.750, reverse 10.959.

REAR AXLE: Hypoid bevel, semi-floating. Ratios: 1200 saloon 4.125:1; 1200 estate 4.444:1; 1500 saloon and estate manual and automatic 3.9:1. Lotus Cortina 3.9:1, note alternative ratios for Lotus model 3.77:1, 4.1:1, 4.43:1.

BRAKES: De Luxe 1200 saloon, front and rear 8in drums, saloons with 1500 engine and all estates front 9in drums, rear 8in drums. GT front 9.5in discs, rear 9in drums, Lotus model, power-assisted, front 9.75in discs, rear 9in drums. De Luxe and Super from 1964, front 9.5in discs, rear 9in drums.

STEERING: Recirculatory ball.

The car at the top is a Lotus Cortina; all others on this page are GT models.

TYRES: 1200 saloon 5.20 x 13, all 1500 saloons 5.60 x 13, all estates and Lotus 6.00 x 13, spare wheel housed in recess to the side of boot in saloons, under rear floor in estates.

SUSPENSION: Front MacPherson struts incorporating independent coil springs and double acting shock absorbers and anti-roll bar, rear semi-elliptic leaf springs with double acting hydraulic shock absorbers. GT rear suspension as above but with trailing radius arms from 1963. Lotus front suspension as above but initially with rear suspension comprising A-frame with coil springs and double acting telescopic shock absorbers, later Lotus as GT model.

DIMENSIONS: Length: 14ft 0.25in (4.273m); **width**: 5ft 2.5in (1.588m); **height**: 4ft 8.5in (1.441m); **wheelbase**: 8ft 2in (2.489m); **track**: front and rear 4ft 1.5in (1.26m); **ground clearance**: 6.5in (16.5cm); **turning circle**: 33ft 9in (10.287m). Estate as saloon except **length**: 14ft 0.5in (4.279m); **height**: 4ft 9.75in (1.464m). Lotus as other saloons except **height**: 4ft 5.75in (1.36m); **track**: front 4ft 3.5in (1.31m), rear 4ft 2.5in (1.28m); **ground clearance**: 5.3in (13.46cm).

APPROXIMATE WEIGHTS: 1200 15cwt 2qtr (788kg), 1500 16cwt (813kg), GT 16cwt 2qtr 22lb (849kg), Lotus 16cwt 2qtr (839kg).

CAPACITIES: Fuel 8 gallons (36.368 litres). Boot saloon 20.9ft^3 (0.592m^3), estate 32.8ft^3 (0.98m^3) or 65.2ft^3 (1.96m^3) with rear seat folded down.

Ford Cortina mark 2

Introduced in October 1966, the mark 2 saloons replaced the mark 1 models. The mark 2 estate did not appear until February 1967, and the mark 2 range was discontinued in September 1970 following the introduction of the mark 3. Although it was based on the mark 1 platform and general running gear, the mark 2 was wider, the increased width allowing for an increase in the front and rear track. Other changes included the universal adoption of front bucket seats across the whole

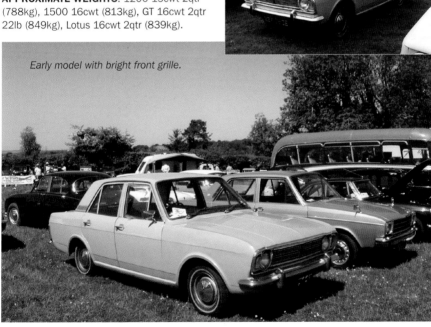

Early model with bright front grille.

range, together with floor-mounted gear change. The handbrake, however, would remain under the dashboard for a little while longer. The fuel tank for saloon models was increased to ten gallons, but estate models remained at eight gallons. There was a new diaphragm spring clutch, and all De Luxe (some Ford brochures use the name de Luxe) and Super models got front disc brakes, and the De Luxe gained additional equipment bringing it more in line with the Super model. The new body lost the sculptured look of the mark 1, and also its unique rear lights, and its appearance was now very similar to the Hillman Hunter, also launched in 1966. Metallic paint became

available for the Cortina, but, unfortunately, it quickly gained a reputation for fading and flaking; the two-tone colour schemes were no longer offered. The new full-width front grille now incorporated all the lights and the

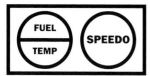

Instrument layout for De Luxe and Super models (left) and GT and 1600E models (right).

Early GT model.

bonnet release. It would be October 1968 before an internal bonnet release was fitted.

Under the bonnet, the 1500 engine was retained, but a 1300 unit based on the 1500 engine replaced the earlier 1200 version. This new engine was the first to use Ford's own carburettor in place of the Solex carburettors previously used. This carburettor was also fitted to the 1500 engine at this time. A new 1600 engine to replace the 1500 came a year later, and featured Ford's new crossflow cylinder head and 'bowl in piston' combustion chambers. This engine would remain in production for many years, being used in a number of different models, including the Escort and Capri.

Other changes to the Cortina mark 2 during its production life included a revised front grille, changes to the GT model's gearbox ratios, the fitting of radial ply tyres to the GT to replace the crossply type, and removal of the radius arms from the rear suspension. Super models got the GT remote control gear change, and the option of reclining front seats on both two- and four-door models. The remote control gear change selector was subsequently changed.

The initial model range comprised two-

This Lotus Cortina has been fitted with a fabric sunroof, a popular conversion before manufacturers offered them as factory-fitted items in glass or metal.

GT model.

and four-door De Luxe 1300 and 1500, Super and GT models. All except the GT were available with optional automatic transmission.

The Lotus model, which was now produced at Dagenham, arrived in March 1967, and a new model, the 1600E, was announced in September 1967, and used components from both the GT and Lotus models, but had a more luxurious interior and extra lights. It was only available as a four-door saloon for the UK market. Other cars to carry the 'E' title included the Zodiac, Corsair, and, eventually,

the Escort. A GT estate was also available for a limited period, and Crayford Engineering produced a convertible version of the Cortina alongside the Corsair convertible. Cortina estates were produced by Ford, and were not converted from saloons by Abbots as the Corsair model had been. Other options offered by Crayford included engine upgrades, but perhaps the most famous engine conversion of the Cortina was the Savage model produced by Race Proved of London, run by Jeff Uren who had previously raced cars for Ford. Generally based on the 1600E model, the conversion consisted of fitting a 3-litre Zodiac engine into the car. This wasn't a simple exercise as it not only involved modifications within the engine compartment but also other changes, such as fitting different rear axle components, relocating the battery to the boot, and changes to the electrical wiring.

Standard equipment for the 1968 De Luxe included temperature gauge, heater, two sun visors, front bucket seats, carpeted floor,

This car is an early 1600E without the black rear panel.

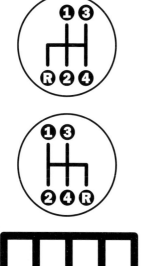

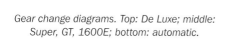

Gear change diagrams. Top: De Luxe; middle: Super, GT, 1600E; bottom: automatic.

All cars on this page are 1600E models.

glove box, half-width front parcel shelf, front door-operated courtesy light, aluminium door scuff plates, childproof locks on rear doors, single stalk on steering column for indicators, main or dipped beam headlights, headlight flasher, single-tone horn. Super added cigarette lighter, different style seating, wider tyres, remote control gear change. GT and 1600E as Super plus ammeter, oil pressure gauge, tachometer (revolution counter), clock, centre console, padded armrest, larger front disc brakes, and radial ply instead of crossply tyres. 1600E, in addition to GT, featured a radio, leather-covered steering wheel, wooden fascia and door cappings, reclining front seats, bucket-style rear seats with centre armrest, black painted grille (body-coloured on early cars), two Wipac auxiliary front driving lights, reversing lights, Rostyle wheels, special badging, pin stripe along the sides, black rear panel, lowered suspension as used for the Lotus model. Optional extras for De Luxe included static seatbelts, 1600cc engine, for Super, inertia reel seatbelts reclining front seats for four-door models, for De Luxe and Super automatic transmission, 1600E had vinyl roof covering. Note that although seatbelts were required by law they were not fitted as standard equipment by many car manufacturers, and incurred an additional charge.

NUMBER PRODUCED: Standard two-door saloon 14,324, four-door 4914, De Luxe two-door saloon 251,537, four-door 347,462, Super two-door 18,950, four-door 116,143, GT two-door 62,592, four-door 54,538, 1600E two-door (export) 2563, four-door 57,254, Lotus 4032, De Luxe and Super estates 90,290.

PRICE WHEN INTRODUCED: De Luxe two-door £706, four-door and Super two-door £730, four-door £755, GT two-door £810, four-door £835. Note above prices increased by £30 in early 1967 when the estate cars were introduced, De Luxe estate £816, Super £890.

COLOURS (1967): Ermine White, Black Cherry, Lagoon, Anchor Blue, Purbeck Grey, Alpine Green, Dragoon Red (GT and 1600E)

Later models with black front grilles.

and metallics, Blue Mink, Silver Fox, Saluki Bronze. Note 1967 brochures state that the Lotus Cortina was available in any of the above colours and not just the familiar white.

ENGINE (1966): Four-cylinder, OHV, De Luxe bore 80.97mm, stroke 61.99mm, 1298cc (79.2in³), maximum bhp 53.5 at 5000rpm, Ford GPD carburettor. Super (optional for De Luxe), bore 80.97mm, stroke 72.8mm, 1498cc (91.5in³), maximum bhp 61 at 4700rpm, Ford GPD carburettor. GT as Super except, maximum bhp 78 at 5200rpm, Weber 28/36 DCD carburettor. Lotus Cortina, four-cylinder, DOHC, bore 82.5mm, stroke 72.75mm, 1558cc (95.07in³), maximum bhp 109 at 6000rpm, two Weber 40DCOE2 carburettors.

ENGINE (1967): Four-cylinder, OHV, De Luxe bore 80.97mm, stroke 61.99mm, 1298cc (79.2in³), maximum bhp 58 at 5000rpm, Super (optional for De Luxe), bore 80.97mm, stroke 77.62mm, 1599cc (97.6in³), maximum bhp 71 at 5000rpm. GT as Super except maximum bhp 88 at 5200rpm, Weber 28/36 DCD carburettor.

GEARBOX: Four-speed, all-synchromesh, floor-mounted gear change. 1300 ratios: top 4.125, 3rd 5.825, 2nd 9.884, 1st 14.615, reverse 16.347. Automatic: top 3.90, 2nd 5.96, 1st 9.45, reverse 8.59. 1500 ratios: top 3.90, 3rd 5.507, 2nd 9.344, 1st 13.818, reverse 15.456. Automatic: top 3.90, 2nd 5.66, 1st 9.32, reverse 8.15. 1600 ratios: top 3.90, 3rd 5.448, 2nd 9.334, 1st 13.818, reverse 12.964. GT from 1967: top 3.90, 3rd 5.448, 2nd 7.839, 1st 11.391, reverse 12.964. Lotus ratios: top 3.77, 3rd 5.28, 2nd 7.58, 1st 11.20, reverse 12.52.

REAR AXLE: Hypoid bevel, semi-floating. Ratio: 1300 manual and automatic 4.125:1, 1500 and 1600 manual and automatic 3.9:1. Lotus Cortina 3.77:1.

BRAKES: Front 9.5in discs, rear 8in drums, GT, 1600E, Lotus 9.625in front discs, rear 9in rear drums.

STEERING: Recirculatory ball.

TYRES: De Luxe 1300 saloon, 5.20 x 13, De Luxe and Super 1500 and 1600 saloon and early GT 5.60 x 13, all estates 6.0 x 13, GT, 1600E, Lotus 165 x 13, spare wheel housed in recess to the side of boot in saloons and under the rear floor in estates.

Crayford convertibles. The white car is a GT.

SUSPENSION: Front MacPherson struts incorporating independent coil springs and telescopic shock absorbers and anti-roll bar, rear semi-elliptic leaf springs with double acting hydraulic shock absorbers (lever arm type on estates). GT, 1600E and Lotus rear suspension as above but with trailing radius arms.

DIMENSIONS: Saloon **length:** 14ft 0in (4.267m); **width:** 5ft 4.9in (1.65m); **height:** 4ft 8.5in (1.435m); **wheelbase:** 8ft 2in (2.490m); **track:** front 4ft 4.5in (1.33m), rear 4ft 3in (1.3m); **ground clearance:** 6.5in

GT estate.

(16.5cm); **turning circle**: 30ft 0in (9.1m). Estate as saloon except **length**: 14ft 1.2in (4.303m). 1600E and Lotus as other saloons except **height**: 4ft 7.7in (1.415m); **ground clearance**: 5.15in (13.1cm).
APPROXIMATE WEIGHTS (FOUR-DOOR SALOONS): 1300, 17cwt 1qtr 11lb (970kg), 1600, 17cwt 2qtr 1lb (890kg), GT 17cwt 3qtr 3lb (904kg), 1600E 17cwt 3qtr 4lb (906kg). **CAPACITIES**: Fuel saloon 10 gallons (45.5 litres), estate 8 gallons (36.4 litres). Boot saloon 20.9ft^3 (0.592m^3), estate 43.3ft^3 (1.225m^3) or 70.5ft^3 (1.995m^3) with rear seat folded down.

Cortina mark 2. A GT model with non-standard wheels.

Ford Zephyr and Zodiac mark 3

Introduced in April 1962, the mark 3 cars, with their angular design, were completely different in appearance from the earlier, curvier mark 1 and 2 cars. The initial design for the mark 3 had been developed by the Italian company Frua, but then it was passed to Roy Brown and his team based in England who retained some of the Frua ideas, such as the curved side windows. The Consul name was discontinued, with the four-cylinder car now being called the Zephyr 4, and the reintroduced Zephyr 6 name used on the mark 1 six-cylinder models. The Zodiac retained its position as the top of the range model, and featured a front grille with slatted area at the top and horizontal bright metal mouldings on the rear panel, as well as gold lettering reminiscent of the mark 2 models. New, however, were four headlights and separate rear quarter lights incorporated in the bodywork instead of the doors. These features were unique to the Zodiac, with the Zephyr retaining two headlights and quarter lights in the rear doors.

Gone were the convertible models, but the estates continued to be made by the coachbuilder Abbots of Farnham, but now appeared without the 'add on' look of the previous models. All estates used the Zodiac bodyshell with its simpler rear doors without quarter lights.

Also gone were the vacuum-operated windscreen wipers and two-tone colour schemes. However, all models gained four-speed all-synchromesh gearboxes with steering column or optional floor-mounted gear

Zephyr 4.

change. The engines were generally the same as those used in the mark 2, but had higher compression ratios and larger carburettors to increase power. The fuel filler cap remained hidden behind the rear number plate.

The Zodiac was the first model to appear, just a few weeks ahead of the Zephyr models, but the estate models were not available until six months later. An additional model, the Executive, which was a more fully-equipped Zodiac, appeared in 1965.

Changes to the interior of all models occurred in 1963, with the lower sections of the Zodiac doors being trimmed with carpet. This change resulted in the stowage bins being replaced by elasticated pockets in the side trim ahead of the doors. External changes to the Zodiac included new overriders with rubber inserts, and reversing lights incorporated into the rear bumper. Standard equipment for the Zephyr 6 included water temperature gauge, two-speed electric wipers, carpeted floor, armrests on all doors, front centre folding armrest, lockable glove box, front parcel shelf, padded dashboard top, front-door-operated courtesy lights. Zodiac added heater, clock, vanity mirror on passenger sun visor, cigar lighter, headlight flasher, windscreen washers, opening rear quarter lights, map pockets, rear

seat centre armrest, courtesy light operated by front and rear doors, overriders with rubber inserts, four headlights. Optional extras include a radio. Executive standard equipment, in addition to Zodiac, included radio with front and rear speakers, individual front seats, front seatbelts, automatic transmission, wing mirrors, front fog and spot lights, locking fuel cap, carpeted boot. Zephyr optional extras included heater, windscreen washers (both standard equipment after 1964), individual fully reclining front seats, leather upholstery, rear seat centre armrest, and overdrive or automatic transmission.

Dashboard layout for the Zephyr.

Zephyr 6.

NUMBER PRODUCED: Zephyr 4 saloon 104,511, estate 725, Zephyr 6 saloon 105,058, estate 1948, Zodiac saloon 75,674, estate 1649.

PRICE WHEN INTRODUCED: Saloons, Zephyr 4 £847, Zephyr 6 £929, Zodiac £1071, estates Zephyr 4 £1172, Zephyr 6 £1245, Zodiac £1387.

COLOURS: All cars, Black Cherry, Ebony, Ermine White, Velvet Blue, Aqua Blue, Purbeck Grey, Spruce Green, Alpina Green, Zephyr and Zodiac only Savoy Black, Caribbean Turquoise, Sapphire Blue, Ambassador Blue, Ascot Grey, Windsor Grey, Platinum Grey, Goodwood Green, Lime Green, Panama Yellow, Imperial Maroon, Monaco Red, Zodiac and Executive only, Midnight Blue, Sable and metallics, Alcuda Blue, Malabu Gold.

ENGINE: Zephyr 4, four-cylinder, OHV, bore 82.55mm, stroke 79.5mm, 1703cc ($103.9in^3$), maximum bhp 68 at 4800rpm, Zenith 36VN carburettor. Zephyr 6, six-cylinder, OHV, bore 82.55mm, stroke 79.5mm, 2553cc ($155.8in^3$) maximum bhp 98 at 4750rpm, Zenith 36WIA-2 carburettor. Zodiac as Zephyr 6 except maximum bhp 109 at 4800rpm,

Zephyr 4 grille, fog lights are an optional extra.

Zephyr 6.

Zodiac.

Gear change diagrams, left manual, right automatic.

A Zephyr 6, identified by its split front grille.

Zenith 41WIA-2 carburettor. Note bhp figures are for models with standard high compression engines of 8.3:1, low compression engines of 7.0:1 were available as an option.

GEARBOX: Four-speed, all-synchromesh, steering column gear change with floor-mounted gear change as an option: Ratios: Zephyr 4, top 3.90, 3rd 5.87, 2nd 9.17, 1st 17.21, reverse 18.20; with optional Borg-Warner automatic gearbox, top 3.55, 2nd 5.15, 1st 8.49, reverse 7.42; Zephyr 6 and Zodiac: top 3.55, 3rd 5.01, 2nd 7.97, 1st 11.23, reverse 11.88, with optional Borg-Warner automatic gearbox, top 3.55, 2nd 5.15, 1st 8.49, reverse 7.42

REAR AXLE: Hypoid bevel, three-quarter floating. Ratios: Zephyr 4, 3.90:1 manual gearbox, 3.545:1 automatic, 4.111 overdrive. Zephyr 6 and Zodiac 3.545:1 with manual, automatic and overdrive gearboxes.

BRAKES: Girling, power-assisted, front 9.75in discs, rear 9in drums, Zephyr 4 rear brake shoe width 1.75in, Zephyr 6 and Zodiac 2.25in. Handbrake under dashboard.

STEERING: Burman recirculating ball.

TYRES: 6.40 x 13.

SUSPENSION: Front, MacPherson, independent, coil springs, telescopic shock

The cars on this page are Zodiac models.

absorbers and anti-roll bar, rear semi-elliptic with double acting lever type shock absorbers.
DIMENSIONS: Zephyr, **length**: 15ft .05in (4.585m); **width**: 5ft 9in (1.753m); **height**: 4ft 9.5in (1.461m); **wheelbase**: 8ft 11in (2.718m); **track**: front 4ft 5in (1.346m), rear 4ft 4in (1.321m); **ground clearance**: 6.8in (17.27cm); **turning circle**: 37ft 10in (11.53m), rear track was increased to 4ft 5.5in (1.359m) from late 1962. Zodiac as Zephyr except **length**: 15ft 2.5in (4.636m).
APPROXIMATE WEIGHTS: Zephyr 4 1ton 3cwt (1155kg), Zephyr 6 1ton 4cwt 2qtr (1244kg), Zodiac 1ton 5cwt 1qtr (1283kg), Executive 1ton 5cwt 1qtr 5lb (1286kg).
CAPACITIES: Fuel 12 gallons (54.5 litres). Boot saloon 21.75ft^3 (0.616m^3), estate 34.6 (0.979m^3) or 64.5 (1.826m^3) with rear seat folded down.

Ford Zephyr, Zodiac, Executive mark 4

Codenamed Panda the mark 4 range was introduced in April 1966 and discontinued in December 1971. The idea, however, of developing a car capable of accommodating a V formation engine had commenced even before the mark 3 models had been launched. As well as V4 and V6 engines,

the mark 4 featured other innovations, such as mounting the spare wheel in the engine compartment to free up space in the boot. Also new were disc brakes all round and the adoption of identical bodyshells for both Zephyr and Zodiac models. The Zodiac and Executive featured four headlights and decorative rear trim incorporating a reflective strip to join the rear lights. The Executive version had more brightwork, and, for the first time since the introduction of the Zodiac in 1953, it was fitted with a larger engine than the six-cylinder Zephyr model.

The overall dimensions of the mark 4 were greater than the mark 3, and it also had a longer wheelbase and wider front and rear track. Other changes over the mark 3 included a new steering column, adjustable for height, and Ford's Aeroflow ventilation system with circular adjustable fresh air vents each end of the dashboard and extractor vents in the rear quarter panels. Gone, however, were the front opening quarter lights, and the estate models, which continued to be produced by Abbots of Farnham, now featured a vinyl roof covering. Once again it appeared like the rear section had just been added on, as per the mark 1 and 2 models, rather than having the mark 3 model's more integrated appearance. Circular

instrument dials replaced the ribbon type that had appeared in the mark 2 and 3 cars, and there was a larger fuel tank. The handbrake remained under the dashboard, although other Ford models had adopted a floor-mounted type.

The standard manual and automatic gear change were also still of the steering column type, with floor-mounted as an option for both types of transmission. Changes to the gearbox included the Borg-Warner automatic transmission and overdrive being replaced by a Ford USA C4 automatic gearbox and Laycock overdrive. The solid beam rear axle assembly

V6, identified by V badges on bonnet and boot.

was replaced by a swing axle layout consisting of a separate differential housing, with drive shafts connected to it using universal joints similar to those used on front-wheel drive cars to connect the gearbox to the wheels. The Zephyr V6 originally had a 3.9:1 rear axle ratio, but this was changed to the 3.7:1 of all the other cars in 1968.

Early cars suffered from engine oil flow problems, and changes to the engine cooling systems occurred in early 1969. By late 1969, Zodiac and Executive models had received wheelarch and bodyside trim. There were also modifications to the rear suspension at various times throughout the life of the mark 4 cars.

Models at launch were Zephyr V4, Zephyr V6, Zodiac and Executive saloons. The Zephyr and Zodiac estates appeared in October 1966, and De Luxe versions of the Zephyrs, which featured a mock front grille, appeared in October 1967.

Standard equipment for the 1970 Zephyr V4 models included: fuel and water temperature gauges, with warning lights for oil pressure and ignition in a single instrument display; heater and ventilation equipment; two-speed wipers, windscreen washers, headlight flasher, indicators and horn were controlled by single steering column stalk; the headlight

dipswitch remained floor-mounted; bench front seat in PVC; carpeted floor; lockable glove box; front-door-operated courtesy light; armrests/door pulls on all doors; two coat hooks; adjustable steering column; interior bonnet release; power-assisted disc brakes. Zephyr V6 added an armrest in the front seat, both De Luxe models added bright metal grille, bonnet top motif, non-reclining front bucket seats with floor-mounted gear change, centre console with padded top and glove box, 14in wheels instead of 13in. Zodiac, in addition to standard Zephyrs, had tachometer, oil pressure gauge, ammeter, clock, instrument housing with burr walnut insert, courtesy lights operated by all doors, vanity mirror on passenger sun visor, dipping style rear view mirror, heated rear window, reclining front bucket seats,

Zephyr De Luxe with (main photo) decorative, non-functional front grille.

centre console with padded top and map compartment, rear seat centre armrest, two rear passenger grab/assist straps, power-assisted steering, reversing lights, bright metal wheelarch mouldings, body side moulding with rubber insert, overriders. Executive model, in addition to Zodiac, had radio with twin loudspeakers, telescopic radio aerial, walnut finish panel to passenger side fascia and door cappings, leather-trimmed seats, inertia reel front seat belts, two front driving lights mounted under the bumper in addition to the four headlights, two wing mirrors, engine compartment light, automatic transmission, metal sliding sunroof.

Optional extras for the Zephyr included radio, front seat armrest, inertia reel seatbelts, heated rear window, reversing lights, 14in wheels, automatic transmission with steering column gear change. For Zephyr V6, overdrive and power steering, and for De Luxe models reclining instead of fixed front bucket seats and the option of either steering column or floor-mounted automatic gear change. Zodiac options were radio, bench-style front seat, automatic transmission or overdrive.

The above car is an early Zodiac without wheelarch and side trim. The car below is a later Zodiac with full trim.

NUMBER PRODUCED: Zephyr V4 41,386, Zephyr V6 61,031, Zodiac and Executive 46,846.

PRICE WHEN INTRODUCED: Zephyr V4 £933, Zephyr V6 £1005, Zodiac £1228, overdrive £54 and automatic transmission £103.

PRICE IN OCTOBER 1969: Zephyr V4 £1027, Zephyr V6 £1115, Zephyr V4 De Luxe £ 1110, Zephyr V6 De Luxe £1197, Zodiac £1477, Executive £1795.

COLOURS: Black Cherry, Ebony, Ermine White, Lagoon Blue, Anchor Blue, Seafoam Blue, Diamond Blue, Marine Blue, Light Blue, Purbeck Grey, Alpina Green, Spruce Green, Light Green, Beige, Burgundy Red, Garnet and the following metallics: Silver Fox, Blue Mink, Saluki Bronze, Amber Gold, Aquatic Jade. All estate cars, Ermine White, Anchor Blue, Diamond Blue, Purbeck Grey, Alpina Green, Garnet. In addition to above Zodiac and Executive saloons only, Aubergine and

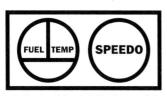

Instrument layout, Zephyr models.

Below: instrument layout, Zodiac and Executive models

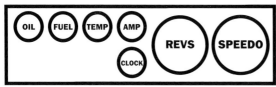

Gear change diagram.

Cars on this page are Executive models.

the following metallics: Venetian Gold, Light Orchid.

COLOURS (1970): Zodiac and Executive, Ermine White, Light Grey, Garnet, Diamond Blue, Anchor Blue and metallics, Silver Fox, Sapphire Blue, Glacier Blue, Pacific Blue, Fern Green, Evergreen, Tawny.

ENGINE: Zephyr V4, four-cylinder, OHV, bore 93.663mm, stroke 72.415mm, 1996cc (121.8in^3), maximum bhp 93 at 4750rpm, Zenith 36IVT carburettor. Zephyr V6, six-cylinder, OHV, bore 93.663mm, stroke 60.35mm, 2495cc (152.2in^3) maximum bhp 118.5 at 4750rpm, Zenith 38IVT carburettor. Zodiac/Executive, six-cylinder, OHV, bore 93.663mm, stroke 72.415mm, 2994cc (182.7in^3), maximum bhp 144 at 4750rpm, Weber dual choke 40DFA carburettor.

GEARBOX: Four-speed, all-synchromesh, steering column or floor-mounted gear change dependent on model: Ratios: Zephyr V4 top 3.70, 3rd 5.569, 2nd 8.706, 1st 16.324, reverse 17.249; Zephyr V6 and Zodiac top 3.70, 3rd 5.224, 2nd 8.192, 1st 11.703, reverse 12.38; early Zephyr V6 top 3.9, 3rd 5.507, 2nd 8.635, 1st 12.36, reverse 13.05.

REAR AXLE: Hypoid bevel. Ratios all models: 3.7:1, early Zephyr V6 3.9:1.

BRAKES: Girling, power-assisted, front 9.63in discs, rear 10in discs.

Above & below a Zodiac estate produced by Abbots of Farnham.

STEERING: Recirculatory ball, Hydrosteer power-assisted on Zodiac and Executive.
TYRES: Zephyr V4 saloon 6.40 x 13, Zephyr V6 saloon and Zephyr V4 and V6 estate 6.70 x 13, all other saloons and estate 185 x 14.
SUSPENSION: Front, MacPherson, coil springs, track control arms, telescopic shock absorbers and anti-roll bar, rear independent coil springs, semi-trailing arms, swinging shackles and telescopic shock absorbers.
DIMENSIONS: Zephyr, **length**: 15ft 5in (4.7m); **width**: 5ft 11.3in (1.81m); **height**: 4ft 8.6in (1.437m); **wheelbase**: 9ft 7in (2.92m);

track: front 4ft 9in (1.45m), rear 4ft 9.5in (1.47m); **ground clearance**: 5.9in (15cm); turning circle: 39ft (11.9m). Zodiac and Executive as above except **length**: 15ft 5.8in (4.72m).
APPROXIMATE WEIGHTS: Zephyr V4 1ton 4cwt 1qtr (1232kg), Zephyr V6 1ton 5cwt 3qtr (1309kg), Zodiac 1ton 5cwt 3qtr 14lb (1315kg), Executive 1ton 6cwt (1322kg).
CAPACITIES: Fuel 15 gallons (68.3 litres). Boot saloon 20.5ft³ (0.58m³), estate 43ft³ (1.21m³) or 82.2ft³ (2.33m³) with rear seat folded down.

Compare the rear lights of the Zodiac above with the Zephyr on page 63.

Ford Escort mark 1

Introduced in January 1968 as a two-door saloon, an estate followed in March 1968, and four-door saloons appeared in October 1969. The Escort, which was advertised as 'The small car that isn't,' was a direct replacement for the Anglia, and was the first Ford designated as an European model and built in factories in Halewood, England, and Saarlouis, Germany. The Escort name, which was used for all markets across the world, had previously been used for an estate car based on a mid 1950s Anglia model. The Escort featured an all-new crossflow engine, with the inlet manifold on one side and the exhaust manifold on other. The valves were positioned so that they were spaced across the top of the cylinder instead of side-by-side, thus allowing an easier flow of gases. A recess shaped as a bowl in the top of the piston served as a combustion chamber instead of being in the cylinder head. This engine, with its five-bearing crankshaft and new style of cylinder head, was referred to as the Kent engine, and was available in 1098cc and 1298cc form. Also available was the Lotus twin-cam 1558cc engine that had been used in the Ford Lotus Cortina, though the Escort version was called the Escort Twin-cam not the Ford Lotus Escort.

Other mechanical changes from the

Anglia included the change to rack and pinion steering, revised MacPherson front suspension without an anti-roll bar, front disc brakes on certain models, and all models now having an all-synchromesh gearbox. The curvaceous shape of the Escort was referred to as 'Coke bottle style,' a descriptive term also applied to the Cortina mark 3. Other styling cues for the Escort included the unique 'dog-bone' shaped front grille, which featured round or rectangular headlights according to model.

Models launched during 1968 included a base model saloon, which was not included in sales brochures as it was aimed primarily at fleet buyers, Deluxe 1100, Super 1100 and 1300, GT 1300 and Twin-cam saloons, Deluxe 1100 and 1300 estates. The Super estate joined the range in May 1969 just ahead of the four-door saloons. The range featuring changes to equipment was renamed in September 1970 and included 1100 L

and 1300 L two- and four-door saloons and two-door estate, 1300 XL two- and four-door saloons and two-door estate, 1300 GT two- and four-door saloon and Twin-cam two-door saloon.

The Escort Mexico, featuring a 1598cc engine, arrived in November 1970. It was produced alongside the short-lived RS 1600 which used a Cosworth 16-valve engine. The Twin-cam model was discontinued in April 1971, and another new model, the 1300 Sport, appeared in October 1971. This used the GT model's engine but had less equipment.

The 1300 E arrived in March 1973. In two-door form it was fitted with the 1300 GT engine and instrumentation, and had the flared wheelarches of the Sport model. It also had walnut veneer trim on the dashboard, door and side panel cappings, auxiliary front lights, and a vinyl roof covering. The four-door version did not arrive until May 1974. The final model in the range, the RS 2000, appeared in October 1973. This was fitted with the OHC 2-litre Pinto engine. All models were replaced by the Escort mark 2 in January 1975.

Changes to specifications in October 1968 included interior door handles and window winders intended to break off in the event of a sudden impact. Super and GT were given, according to the colour of

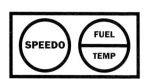

Instrument layouts: Super (above) and GT (below).

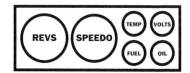

upholstery, colour-coded steering wheel and column shroud, front ashtray, heater panel and Aeroflow vents, and simulated woodgrain was added to the dashboard. Changes in late 1970 included revisions to the engines and improvements to interiors of some models. Standard equipment for the 1968 Deluxe included heater, Aeroflow ventilation system, padded fascia top, parcel shelf, two sun visors, individual front bucket seats, colour-keyed rubber floor mats, foot-operated windscreen washers, headlight flasher, door-operated courtesy light, aluminium door scuff plates, and round headlights. Super, in addition to Deluxe, had water temperature gauge, cigarette lighter, carpet instead of rubber floor mats, different seats, mat in luggage boot, wheel trim rings and other exterior trim, rectangular instead of round headlights. GT, in addition to Super, had front disc brakes with power-assistance, large instrument binnacle incorporating speedometer, tachometer, fuel, water temperature and oil pressure gauges, battery condition indicator gauge, and radial instead of crossply tyres. Standard equipment for 1972 L model, in addition to 1968 Deluxe, included two-speed wipers, carpet instead of rubber floor mats, map pocket, passenger grab handles, coat hooks, opening rear quarter lights on two-door models, boot light, reversing lights, hazard flashers. XL, in addition to L

and previous Super model, had vanity mirror on passenger sun visor, instrument binnacle as 1968 GT model, and overriders. Sport, in addition to XL, had wide front wheelarches to accommodate larger wheels – 13in instead of 12in – front disc brakes with power-assistance, black finish to the fascia, front quarter bumpers, black-painted rear end panel, spare

All cars on this page are Mexico models.

wheel located on boot floor instead of to the side. Note that the Sport was available as a two-door model only. GT was as XL model plus special sports steering wheel, front disc brakes with power-assistance, and black-painted rear end panel. Optional extras for 1968 models included, for Deluxe and Super, front disc brakes with power-assistance, wide rim wheels with radial tyres, automatic transmission, leather-rimmed sports steering wheel, inertia reel seatbelts, radio, metallic paint. Additional equipment for the Twin-cam for competition use included two 9-gallon fuel tanks, magnesium sump shield, limited-slip differential, adjustable telescopic shock absorbers, fibreglass bonnet and boot lid.

NUMBER PRODUCED: Two-door 611,305, four-door 153,660, estate 130,908, van 186,599, RS and Mexico 15,277.
PRICE WHEN INTRODUCED: Saloons: 1100 Deluxe £713, 1300 Super £773, GT £851. Estate: 1100 Deluxe £796. Later (1970) saloons: 1100 L two-door £832, 1300 L four-door £896, 1300 GT two-door £966. Estate: 1100 L £928.
COLOURS (1968): Ermine White, Light Green, Anchor Blue, Light Blue, Red, Beige and metallics, Blue Mink, Saluki Bronze, Aquatic Jade, Silver Fox.
COLOURS (1972): Diamond White, Le Mans Green, Daytona Yellow, Monza Blue, Marine Blue, Sebring Red, Sunset, Burgundy Red, Copper Brown and metallics, Fern Green, Evergreen, Sapphire, Pearl Grey, Tawny.
ENGINE: Four-cylinder, OHV (except Twin-cam, RS and Mexico models), 1100, bore 80.993mm, stroke 53.289mm, 1098cc (66.98in^3), maximum bhp 53 at 5500rpm, Ford 30mm carburettor (Ford 32mm from October 1970). 1300, bore 80.993mm, stroke 62.992mm, 1298cc (79.2in^3), maximum bhp 61.5 at 5000rpm, Ford 34mm carburettor.

Gear change layout.

All cars on this page are 1300 E models.

GT and Sport as 1300 except maximum bhp 75 at 6000rpm, special high lift camshaft, Weber 32DFE carburettor (Weber 32DGV from October 1970). Twin-cam, DOHC, bore 82.55mm, stroke 72.882mm, 1558cc (95.05in³), maximum bhp 115 at 6000rpm, two Weber 40DCOE carburettors. RS 1600, DOHC, bore 80.97mm, stroke 77.6mm, 1601cc (97.7in³), maximum bhp 120 at 6500rpm, two Weber 40DCOE carburettors. Mexico, OHC, bore 80.98mm, stroke 77.72mm, 1598cc (97.5in³), maximum bhp 86.9 at 5500rpm, Weber 32DFM carburettor. RS 2000, OHC, bore 90.82, stroke 76.95mm, 1993cc (121.6in³), maximum bhp 100 at 5750rpm, Weber 32/36 carburettor.

This estate belonged to the author's father.

GEARBOX (1968): Four-speed, all-synchromesh, 1100 and 1300 Deluxe and Super saloons ratios: top 3.9, 3rd 5.558, 2nd 8.522, 1st 14.258, reverse 16.517. 1300 GT ratios: top 4.125, 3rd 5.849, 2nd 8.229, 1st 13.765, reverse 15.951. Estate 1100 ratios: top 4.44, 3rd 6.327, 2nd 9.701, 1st 16.233, reverse 18.503. 1300 ratios: top 4.125, 3rd 5.878, 2nd 9.013, 1st 15.081, reverse 17.469. Twin-cam ratios: top 3.777, 3rd 5.276, 2nd 7.592, 1st 11.225, reverse 12.555.

REAR AXLE (1968): Hypoid bevel, semi-floating. Ratios: 1100 and 1300 Deluxe and Super saloons 3.9:1, 1300 GT 4.125:1, 1100 estates 4.44:1, 1300 estates 4.125:1, Twin-cam standard 3.777:1 with alternatives for competition use of 4.71:1, 5.1:1, 5.5:1.

1300 Es (above), RS2000 (below).

GEARBOX (1972): Four-speed, all-synchromesh, floor-mounted gear change, 1100 and 1300 L and XL saloons and 1300 estate. Ratios: top 3.89, 3rd 5.54, 2nd 8.499, 1st 14.222, reverse 16.474. 1300 GT ratios: top 3.89, 3rd 5.516, 2nd 7.761, 1st 12.98, reverse 15.047. Sport ratios: top 4.11, 3rd 5.828, 2nd 8.199, 1st 13.715, reverse 15.897. Estate 1100 ratios: as 1968 estate 1300.

REAR AXLE (1972): Hypoid bevel, semi-floating. Ratios: 1100 and 1300 L, XL and 1300 GT 3.89:1; Sport 4.11; 1100 estate 4.125; 1300 estate 3.89:1.

BRAKES: Girling, 1100 and 1300 Deluxe, Super, L, XL saloons and 1100 estate, front and rear 8in drums, 1300 estate, GT, Sport, power-assisted, front 8.6in discs, rear 8in drums, Mexico and Twin-cam, power-assisted front 9.625in discs, rear 9in drums.

STEERING: Rack and pinion.

TYRES: 1100 and 1300 Deluxe and Super saloons 5.50 x 12, GT 155 x 12, all estates

6.00 x 12, 1100 and 1300 L and XL saloons 5.50 x 12, Twin-cam, RS, Mexico, Sport saloons 165 x 13.

SUSPENSION: Front MacPherson struts incorporating independent coil springs and telescopic shock absorbers, rear semi-elliptic leaf springs and hydraulic double acting shock absorbers.

DIMENSIONS: **Length**: saloons 13ft 0.6in (3.978m); **width**: 5ft 1.8in (1.57m); **height**: 4ft 5in (1.346m); **wheelbase**: 7ft 10.5in (2.4m); **track**: front 4ft 1in (1.245m), rear 4ft 2in (1.27m); **ground clearance**: 6.5in (16.5cm); **turning circle**: 29ft 8.4in (9.05m); estates as saloons except **length**: 13ft 4.8in (4.08m).

APPROXIMATE WEIGHTS: 1100 Deluxe two-door 14cwt 2qtr 18lb (746kg), 1300 E four-door 16cwt 0qtr 5lb (815kg), RS2000 18cwt (915kg).

CAPACITIES: Fuel 9 gallons (40.95 litres), boot saloon 15ft^3 (0.806m^3), estate 31ft^3 (1.649m^3) or 54ft^3 (2.87m^3) with rear seat folded down.

Ford Escort mark 2

Introduced in January 1975 to replace the mark 1 Escort, the range was extended in July 1975 to include Popular and Popular Plus models. Project Brenda, as the mark 2 was codenamed, had a more angular appearance, with a 23 per cent larger glass area. It also featured improved vents for the Aeroflow system. The estate car, although it had the revised frontal treatment, retained the mark 1 estate bodywork from the A-pillars backwards. The range was considerably increased from the mark 1, and, from the start, included 1100, 1300 and 1600 engines, with L, GL and Ghia models replacing L, XL and the 1300 E. Various sporting models were introduced at different stages, including the RS1800, available for only a short period, and with body colour limited to Diamond White. There was also the RS 2000, with its unique front nose cone manufactured from polyurethane and fitted with four headlights. Although developed in England, the RS 2000 and RS Mexico models were manufactured in Saarlouis, Germany.

1.6 Ghia models.

The range in July 1975 included 1100 two-door Popular, Popular Plus, L, estate and four-door Popular Plus and L. 1300 two-door Popular, Popular Plus, L, Sport. L and GL estates, four-door Popular Plus, L, GL, and Ghia models. 1600 Sport two-door and Ghia four-door.

Special editions started to appear from 1978 onward. These included the Capital, Linnet, Harrier, Goldcrest saloons, and the Huntsman estate. The arrival of 'special editions' in the Ford range often appeared to signal that a completely new model, ie the Escort mark 3, was about to be introduced.

At various stages during its life, there were improvements and upgrades made to various models, such as the change to 13in wheels and front disc brakes on some of the lesser models, revision of the rear suspension to feature only a single leaf rear spring, and changed damper settings. The introduction of wider wheels marginally increased track width, and changes to appearance included the adoption of black front radiator grilles for some models, and fitting the L models with rectangular headlights and bodyside mouldings. The Popular Plus gained coachlines, and benefited from a heated rear window. Standard equipment for the Popular included a water temperature gauge, heater with two-speed fan, Aeroflow ventilation system, two-speed windscreen

Photographed in the mid 1980s, this was the author's mark 2 Escort 1.3 GL.

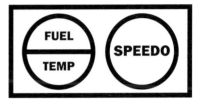

Instrument layout, Popular model.

1.3 L.

wipers, electrically operated windscreen washers (mark 1 Escort had manually operated windscreen washers), headlight flasher, ignition/steering lock, individual front bucket seats, driver's side front parcel shelf, rubber floor matting, aluminium door scuff plates, interior bonnet release, black-painted bumpers, door handles and window surrounds. Popular Plus had carpet instead of rubber floor covering, full-width front parcel tray, different trim, dipping rear view mirror, reversing lights, radial ply tyres. L, in addition to Popular Plus, came with bright bumpers, door handles and window surrounds, heated rear window, reclining front seats, grab handles/coat hooks, and hazard warning flashers. GL added a vanity mirror on the passenger sun visor, soft feel fascia trim, centre console with clock, illuminated cigarette lighter, armrests, fully trimmed doors and quarter panels, chrome gearshift lever, rubber bumper inserts, bodyside moulding, square Halogen headlights instead of circular semi-sealed units, boot light. Ghia, in addition to GL, had tachometer, real wood veneer on the fascia, soft-feel

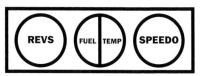

Instrument layout, Sport models.

rimmed steering wheel, glove box, integral headrests on front seats, overriders, black vinyl roof, black window surrounds, bright exhaust trim, tinted glass, power-assisted brakes, carpeted boot. Sport equipment generally as

The car at the top is a 1.3 Ghia; the estate is a 1.3 L.

L model but with tachometer, trip mileage recorder, headrests on non-reclining front seats, no grab handles, sports steering wheel, front quarter bumpers and rear bumpers with overriders all finished in black, black finished window surrounds, two door-mounted rear view mirrors, two halogen circular headlights, and two auxiliary halogen driving lights.

Optional extras, where not fitted as standard equipment, included headrests, hazard warning flashers, heated rear window, Halogen headlights, *door-mounted mirror, *vinyl roof, *tinted glass, (*not Popular or Popular Plus).

NUMBER PRODUCED: UK approximately 960,000.

PRICES (1975): Saloons: 1100 two-door Popular £1349, four-door, L £1655, 1300 two-door, Popular £1416, Sport £1873, four-door L £1703, Ghia £2156, 1600 two-door, Sport £1933, four-door, Ghia £2216. Estates: 1300 L £1703, GL £1998.

COLOURS (1978): Diamond White, Riviera Blue, Midnight Blue, Calypso Green, Venetian Red, Sierra Beige, Tuscan Beige, Signal Orange, Signal Yellow and metallics, Strato Silver, Cosmos Blue, Jupiter Red, Oyster Gold, Roman Bronze. Vinyl roof available in Black or Tobacco according to main body colour and interior trim.

ENGINE (1977): Four-cylinder, OHV (except Mexico and RS models), 1100 economy, bore 80.98mm, stroke 53.289mm, 1098cc (66.98in^3), maximum bhp 41 at 5300rpm, Ford 30mm carburettor. Note early standard 1100 engine for L model maximum bhp 48 at 5500rpm, Ford 32mm carburettor. 1300, bore 80.98mm, stroke 62.992mm, 1296cc (79.08in^3), maximum bhp 57 at 5500rpm, Ford 34 mm carburettor. Sport and Ghia as 1300 except maximum bhp 70 at 5500rpm, Weber twin-choke 32DGV carburettor. 1600, bore 80.98mm, stroke 77.62mm, 1598cc (97.5in^3), maximum bhp 84 at 5500rpm, Weber 32/32DGV carburettor. RS Mexico, OHC, bore 87.65mm, stroke 66mm, 1593cc (97.2in^3), maximum bhp 95 at 5750rpm, Weber 32/36DGAV carburettor. RS 1800, DOHC, bore 86.75mm, stroke 77.62mm, 1834cc (111.9in^3), maximum bhp 115 at

The cars on this page are RS2000s.

77

6000rpm, Weber 32/36DGAV carburettor, RS 2000, OHC, bore 90.82mm, stroke 76.95mm, 1993cc (121.6in³), maximum bhp 110 at 5500rpm, Weber 32/36DGAV carburettor.

GEARBOX (1977): Four-speed, all-synchromesh, floor-mounted gear change. 1100 and 1300 ratios: top 3.89, 3rd 5.554, 2nd 8.499, 1st 16.474, reverse 16.517. 1300 Sport and Ghia ratios: top 4.125, 3rd 5.849, 2nd 8.229, 1st 13.765, reverse 15.989. 1600 Sport and Ghia ratios: top 3.54, 3rd 5.02, 2nd 7.062, 1st 11.813, reverse 13.721. RS Mexico and RS2000 ratios: top 3.54, 3rd 4.85, 2nd 6.974, 1st 12.942, reverse 12.94. RS1800 ratios: top 3.54, 3rd 4.46, 2nd 6.372, 1st 11.894, reverse 11.93. Note Sport and Ghia 1300 and 1600 models used same internal ratios but with different rear axle ratio.

REAR AXLE (1977): Hypoid bevel, semi-floating. Ratios: 1100 and 1300 3.89:1, 1300 Sport and Ghia 4.125:1, 1600, Ghis, Sport, RS Mexico, RS1800, RS2000 3.54:1.

BRAKES: Hydraulic dual line, 1100, Popular, Popular Plus and early L models front and rear 8in drums, later 1100 L and all 1300 models, front 9.6in discs, rear 9in drums, Sport, Ghia and RS models as 1300 but power-assisted. Note specifications varied during production.

STEERING: Rack and pinion.

TYRES: 1100 Popular 6 x 12, Popular Plus, L 155 x 12, 1300 Popular Plus, L, GL, Ghia 155 x 13, 1600 Ghia 155 x 13, 1300 Sport 175/70 x 13, 1600 Sport, Mexico 175/70 SR x 13, RS 1800 and RS 2000 175/70 HR x 13. Note 1100 L from July 1975 and Popular models from September 1978 fitted with 155 x 13 tyres.

SUSPENSION: Front MacPherson struts incorporating independent coil springs and telescopic shock absorbers, anti-roll bar, rear semi-elliptic leaf springs and telescopic shock absorbers, rear anti-roll bar on 1300 and 1600 models, trailing radius arms on RS models.

DIMENSIONS: **Length**: saloons without overriders 13ft 0.6in (3.978m), with overriders 13ft 3.8in (4.058m); **width**: 5ft 2.8in (1.596m); **height**: 4ft 7.1in (1.398m); **wheelbase**: 7ft 10.5in (2.4m), **track**: front 4ft 2in (1.27m), rear 4ft 3in (1.295m); **ground clearance**: 5.5in (14cm); **turning circle**: 29ft 2.4in (8.9m), estates as saloons

RS Mexico.

RS2000.

except **length**: without overriders 13ft 3.7in (4.056m), with overriders 13ft 6.8in (4.136m); **width**: 5ft 1.6in (1.564m); **height**: 4ft 7.7in (1.414m).
APPROXIMATE WEIGHTS: 1300 GL 16cwt 2qtr 11lb (843kg), Ghia 17cwt 1qtr 8lb (880kg), 1600 Sport 17cwt 2qtr 20lb (898kg), Ghia 18cwt 0qtr 19lb (923kg).
CAPACITIES: Fuel 9 gallons (40.95 litres), boot saloon 15ft^3 (0.806m^3), estate 31.5ft^3 (1.676m^3) or 54ft^3 (2.873m^3) with rear seat folded down.

Ford Capri mark 1

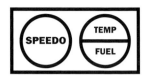

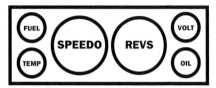

Instrument layouts: L (top), and GT.

Introduced in January 1969 and advertised as 'The car your always promised yourself,' by 1971 it had become 'The car that keeps its promises.' The Capri name had been used on an earlier two-door coupé derived from the Ford Consul Classic. The Classic was discontinued in September 1963, and the Consul Capri was discontinued in July 1964. The *new* Capri had a long life, from 1969 to 1987, without changing its basic shape. It was immediately identifiable, even after the introduction of an opening rear tailgate and the loss of the side swage on the mark 2. By comparison, the Ford Escort introduced in 1968 bore absolutely no resemblance to the 1987 Escort model. Revisions to the Capri were generally mechanical, or to the interior and levels of equipment fitted as standard. The external features that did change a few times, however, were the lights and bumpers. Unlike earlier Fords, which had often been offered as Basic or De Luxe models with a

This is a GT with optional vinyl roof. The Blue car below is a 1600GT XLR.

choice of two different engines, the Capri was offered with three Custom packs: L exterior dress up; X internal refinement; and R sporty dress up. The interior and external packs could be mixed, so with six engine options this enabled buyers to have a choice of thirty two models. This was ultimately trimmed down to L and XL, with a choice of standard or GT engines of varying capacities. The early 1970 range comprised 1300, 1300L, 1300X, 1300XL, 1300GT, 1300GTL, 1300GTX, 1300GTXL, 1300GTR, 1300GTXLR, 1600 models as 1300, 2000GT, 2000GTL, 2000GTX, 2000GTXL, 2000GTR, 2000GTXLR, 3000 models as 2000.

The L pack comprised chrome-plated

Identification badges on front wing.

exhaust trim, lockable fuel cap, bright metal wheel trims, bodyside mouldings and dummy air scoops, overriders with rubber inserts, wash/wipe facility. X pack featured reclining front bucket seats, individual countered rear seats with folding centre armrest, dipping rear view mirror, dual horns, handbrake warning

light, map reading light below fascia, twin reversing lights. R pack included aluminium sports road wheels, padded leather steering wheel with bright metal inserts between padded spokes and rim, two auxiliary driving lights with PVC covers, bright metal bodyside moulding, black front grille, optional matt black bonnet and cowl, lower rear panel and door sills. Standard equipment included heater with two-speed fan, Aeroflow ventilation system, single-speed wipers, foot-operated windscreen washers, loop pile carpet, padded sun visors, door-operated interior light, front parcel shelf, interior bonnet release, sealed beam headlights, chromed front and rear bumpers. GT models added battery condition indicator and oil pressure gauge, tachometer, vanity mirror on passenger sun visor, cigarette lighter, centre console with clock, two-speed instead of single-speed wipers, special door armrests and grab handles, bright metal pedal mouldings, power-assisted brakes (not 1300GT). Optional extras in addition to custom packs included automatic transmission, radio, metallic paint finish, sliding roof, vinyl-covered roof, heated rear window, opening rear quarter lights.

In September 1971 a special edition based on the 2000GT XLR appeared. Available only in Vista Orange, it had a radio, rear window slats, vinyl roof, heated rear

Gear change diagram.

window, special wheel trims, and black boot spoiler.

PRICE WHEN INTRODUCED: 1300L £942, 1600L £988, 1600GTXLR £1162, 2000GTXL £1172, 3000GTXL £1335.

COLOURS (1971): Light Grey, Le Mans Green, Sunset, Electric Blue, Marine Blue, Burgundy Red, Daytona Yellow, Ermine White and metallics Silver Fox, Tawny, Sapphire Blue, Evergreen, Fern Green.

ENGINE: Four-cylinder (except 3000), 1300, OHV, bore 80.98mm, stroke 62.99mm, 1298cc (79.2in^3), maximum bhp 52 at 5000rpm, Ford 34mm carburettor. 1300GT model maximum bhp 64 at 6000rpm, Weber 32DFE carburettor. 1600, OHV, bore 80.98mm, stroke 77.62mm, 1599cc (97.6in^3), maximum bhp 64 at 4800rpm, Ford 36mm carburettor. 1600GT model, maximum bhp 82 at 5400rpm, Weber 32DFM2 carburettor. 2000GT (V4, OHV), bore 93.66mm, stroke 72.44mm, 1996cc (121.8in^3), maximum bhp 92.5 at 5500rpm,

Weber 32/36DFV carburettor. 3000GT (V6, OHV), bore 93.66mm, stroke 72.44mm, 2994cc (182.7in³), maximum bhp 128 at 4750rpm, Weber 40DFAV carburettor.

GEARBOX: Four-speed, all-synchromesh, floor-mounted gear change. Ratios: 1300 and 1300GT, top 4.125, 3rd 5.825, 2nd 9.884, 1st 14.615, reverse 16.347; 1600 top 3.9, 3rd 5.507, 2nd 9.344, 1st 13.818, reverse 15.456; 1600GT top 3.777, 3rd 5.276, 2nd 7.592, 1st 11.225, reverse 12.555; 2000GT top 3.44, 3rd 4.806, 2nd 6.914, 1st 10.224, reverse 11.435; 3000GT top 3.22, 3rd 4.547, 2nd 7.129, 1st 10.185, reverse 10.774.

REAR AXLE: Hypoid bevel, semi-floating. Ratios: 1300 and 1300GT 4.125:1; 1600 3.9:1; 1600GT 3.777:1; 2000GT 3.44:1; 3000GT 3.22:1.

BRAKES: Girling, 1300 front 9.59in discs, rear 8in drums; 1600, 2000 and 3000, front 9.625in discs, rear 9in drums, power-assisted on 1600GT, 2000GT, 3000GT.

STEERING: Rack and pinion, collapsible double-jointed column.

TYRES: 1300 and 1600, 6.00 x 13, 1300GT, 1600GT, 2000GT, 165SR x 13, 3000GT 185HR x 13.

SUSPENSION: Front, MacPherson struts, independent coil springs, track control arms and anti-roll bar, rear semi-elliptic leaf springs, radius arms, double acting hydraulic shock absorbers.

DIMENSIONS: Length: 13ft 11.8in (4.262m); **width:** 5ft 4.8in (1.646m); **height:** 4ft 2.7in (1.288m), GT models 4ft 2.2in (1.275m); **wheelbase:** 8ft 4.75in (2.56m); **track:** front 4ft 5in (1.346m), rear 4ft 2in (1.32m); **ground clearance:** 4.5in (11.5cm); **turning circle:** 32ft (9.75m).

APPROXIMATE WEIGHTS: 1300GT 17cwt 2qtr 25lb (900kg), 1600GT 18cwt 0qtr 14lb (921kg), 2000GT 18cwt 3qtr 15lb (959kg), 3000GT 1ton 3qtr 6lb (1057kg).

CAPACITIES: Fuel 1300, 1600, 2000, 10.5 gallons (48 litres), 3000GT 13.6 gallons (62 litres). Boot 12ft³ (0.34m³).

Ford Capri mark 1 1/2

In September 1972 the mark 1 received a facelift and a new 1600 engine, plus changes to the suspension and revisions to the interior. The changes included larger rectangular headlights, front indicators integrated into the front bumper, larger rear light clusters incorporating reversing lights, smaller imitation vents on the side of the car, bonnet bulge on all models, full-width rear anti-roll bar, redesigned seats with cloth inserts, larger instrument dials, lockable glove box with light instead of front parcel shelf, and more.

The reduced range now comprised 1300L, 1600L, 1600XL, 1600GT, 2000GT, 3000GXL. At the end of 1973 an additional model, the RS3100, was introduced. Standard equipment for the L now included a vanity mirror on the passenger sun visor, simulated wood finish on the fascia, cigarette lighter, armrests on the front doors, two-speed wipers, aluminium scuff plates on the door sills, steering column lock. XL had, in addition to L, reclining front seats, individual bucket-style rear seats, dipping rear view mirror, illuminated heater control panel, two-tone horn, and handbrake warning light. GT, in addition to XL, featured black vinyl fascia covering, centre console unit with gear shift gaiter and glove box, clock, sports steering wheel, tachometer, oil pressure and battery condition gauges. GXL model, which was only available with the 3000cc engine, had twin halogen headlights, different style front grille, bodyside rubbing strip with vinyl insert, heated rear window, rear armrests incorporating ashtrays, cowlside map pockets, radio, opening rear quarter windows, engine compartment and boot lights.

Note: all models except for the 1300 were now fitted with an alternator. Optional for the GT models was a special pack incorporating two auxiliary driving lights, bodyside stripe,

GXL with twin circular headlights.

GT model with non-standard wheels.

sports road wheels, simulated leather gear shift knob, and an adjustable map reading light.

NUMBER PRODUCED (MARK 1 AND 1 1/2): 374,700 UK, 1,209,100 worldwide.
PRICE IN NOVEMBER 1972: 1300L £1123, 1600XL £1243, 1600GT £1370, 2000GT £1400, 3000GXL £1831.
COLOURS (1972): Diamond White, Sebring Red, Sunset, Burgundy Red, Monza Blue, Marine Blue, Le Mans Green, Daytona Yellow and metallics, Fern Green, Evergreen, Sapphire Blue, Pearl Grey, Copper Brown, Tawny.
ENGINE: Four-cylinder (except 3000), 1300, OHV, bore 80.98mm, stroke 62.99mm, 1298cc (79.2in³), maximum bhp 57 at 5500rpm, Ford 34mm carburettor, 1600, OHC, bore 87.65mm, stroke 66mm, 1593cc (97.2in³), maximum bhp 72 at 5500rpm, Ford 36mm carburettor, 1600GT, maximum bhp 88 at 5700rpm, Weber 32/36DGAV carburettor. 2000GT, (V4 OHV), bore 93.66mm, stroke 72.44mm, 1996cc (121.8in³), maximum bhp 92 at 5250rpm, Weber 32/36DFV carburettor. 3000GXL, (V6 OHV), bore 93.66mm, stroke 72.44mm, 2994cc (182.7in³), maximum bhp 140 at 5300rpm, Weber 38/27DGAS carburettor. Note Capris produced in Germany originally had V configuration four-cylinder engines of 1305cc, 1498cc, 1699cc and six-cylinder V engines of 1998cc, 2293cc, 2550cc. The 1300, 1500 and 1700 engines were replaced

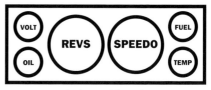

Instrument layout.

by in-line four-cylinder engines of 1293cc and 1593cc in 1972.
GEARBOX: Four-speed, all-synchromesh, floor-mounted gear change. Ratios: 1300, top 4.125, 3rd 5.825, 2nd 9.884, 1st 14.615, reverse 16.347; 1600 top 3.9, 3rd 5.499, 2nd 9.399, 1st 13.806, reverse 15.444; 1600GT top 3.77, 3rd 5.316, 2nd 8.917 1st 13.346, reverse 14.929; 2000 top 3.44, 3rd 4.816, 2nd 6.914, 1st 10.217, reverse 11.421; 3000 top 3.09, 3rd 4.357, 2nd 5.944, 1st 9.764, reverse 10.352.
REAR AXLE: Hypoid bevel, semi-floating. Ratios: 1300 4.125:1; 1600 3.90:1; 1600GT 3.77:1; 2000 3.44:1; 3000 3.09:1.
BRAKES: Front 9.625in discs, rear 9in drums, power-assisted on all models except 1300.
STEERING: Rack and pinion, collapsible double-jointed column.

Gear change diagram.

Left: Note the rear window slats.

Top GT, middle GXL, bottom XL.

TYRES: 1300 6.00 x 13, 1600, 2000, 165SR x 13, 3000 185/70HR x 13.
SUSPENSION: Front, MacPherson struts, independent coil springs, track control arms and anti-roll bar, rear semi-elliptic leaf springs, anti-roll bar, double acting hydraulic shock absorbers.
DIMENSIONS: Length: 13ft 11.8in (4.262m); **width**: 5ft 4.8in (1.646m); **height**: 4ft 2.7in (1.288m), GT models 4ft 2.2in (1.275m); **wheelbase**: 8ft 4.75in (2.56m); **track**: front 4ft 5in (1.346m), rear 4ft 2in (1.32m); **ground clearance**: 4.5in (11.5cm); **turning circle**: 32ft (9.75m).
APPROXIMATE WEIGHTS: 1300 17cwt, 2qtr 24lb (880kg); 1600GT 18cwt 0qtr 8lb (920kg); 2000GT 18cwt 3qtr 15lb (959kg); 3000GXL 1ton 1cwt 1qtr (1079kg).
CAPACITIES: Fuel 1300, 1600, 2000, 10.5 gallons (48 litres), 3000GT 13.6 gallons (62 litres). Boot 12ft³ (0.34m³), 3000GT 7.3ft³ (0.21m³).

Ford Capri mark 2

Introduced in March 1974 with a completely new body incorporating an opening rear tailgate, the sides of the car were now of much plainer appearance, and lost the sculptured swage on the rear wings. The bonnet bulge was now smaller, but the overall dimensions of the car increased. It was, however, still immediately recognisable as a Capri.

With the opening rear tailgate came folding rear seats, and, on the higher specification models, the seats folded individually. Amongst other changes were a larger glass area, with the side windows now dipping down towards the waistline. The rear three-quarter window extended further back, and, with the restyling needed to accommodate the rear tailgate, the rear pillars were now smaller, necessitating moving the petrol filler cap from its original position on the pillar towards the back of the rear wing. Other changes included moving the indicators to the side of the headlights, and the door handles were now recessed.

Mechanical changes included increased rear track, larger front discs and wider rear drums, the Pinto 2.0-litre OHC engine replaced the previous Kent 2.0-litre OHV unit, the

suspension was softened, and power steering became available as an option. There were the customary changes to range availability and levels of equipment within the range.

The range at introduction included 1300L, 1600XL, 1600GT, 2000GT, 2000 Ghia, 3000GT, and 3000 Ghia. In June 1975 a special edition S model appeared. It was based on the various GT models and was only available in Black. Then, in October 1975, XL models were replaced by GL models, with some equipment upgrades, and the 1600 GT and 2000 GT models were renamed as 1600 S and 2000 S. The new S models were now available in a range of colours, not just Black, but they retained the black mirrors and bumpers of the original special edition model, and featured its unique wheels and vinyl-covered seats with fabric inserts.

In February 1978, just prior to the launch of the mark 3, the 1300 engine was revised and fitted with a new carburettor for improved fuel economy. Standard equipment for the 1975 L model included water temperature gauge, heater with two-speed blower, two-speed wipers with electrically operated windscreen washers, glove box, cigarette lighter, ignition/steering column lock, plus headlight flasher, main and dipped beam, indicators and horn all controlled from a stalk mounted on the steering column, carpet in passenger area, rubber mat in luggage compartment, rear compartment cover (parcel tray), individual front bucket seats and one-piece folding bench-type rear seat, interior mirror, door-operated courtesy lights, two padded sun visors with vanity mirror on passenger's visor, interior bonnet release, aluminium scuff plates, heated rear window,

GT model.

driver's door mirror, reversing lights, hazard warning flashers, rubber inserts in bumpers, power-assisted brakes. XL added carpet instead of rubber mat in the luggage compartment, dipping interior mirror, reclining front seats, centre console. GT added tachometer, oil pressure gauge, batter indication meter, split folding rear seat, halogen headlights, larger tyres.

Standard equipment for 1977 models was as follows: 1300 base model now generally as 1975 L model plus intermittent windscreen wiper facility but retained black bumpers, radiator grille, door handles, and window surrounds. L now had wood-effect instrument panel, carpet instead of rubber in the luggage compartment, split folding rear seat. GL, in addition to previous XL, had wood-effect instrument surround, radio, clock. Capri S, in addition to GL, had vinyl/fabric seats with headrests, two door mirrors, special bodyside coachlines, front air dam, power steering on 3-litre model. Ghia model had vinyl roof covering with tilting sunshine roof, tinted glass, remote control driver's door mirror, and more. Optional extras included automatic transmission (not 1300 models, standard on 3000 Ghia), and, where not fitted as standard, vinyl roof, radio, tailgate wash/wipe, headrests, tinted glass, sliding/tilting sunroof, and more.

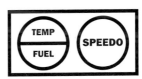

Instrument layout L and GL.

NUMBER PRODUCED: 84,400 UK.
PRICE WHEN INTRODUCED: 1300L £1731, 1600GT £2087, 2000 Ghia £2801, 3000 Ghia automatic £3241. October 1975 prices 1300L £1833, 1600S £2307, 2000GL £2158, 3000S £2549, 3000 Ghia automatic £3371.
COLOURS (1977): Included, Jupiter Red, Nevada Beige, Oyster Gold, Strato Silver, Signal Orange.
ENGINE: Four-cylinder (except 3000), 1300, OHV, bore 80.98mm, stroke 62.99mm, 1298cc (79.2in^3), maximum bhp 57 at 5500rpm, Ford 34mm carburettor. 1600,

Ghia model.

Gear change layout.

OHC, bore 87.65mm, stroke 66mm, 1593cc (97.2in³), maximum bhp 72 at 5200rpm, Ford 36mm carburettor. 1600GT and S model, maximum bhp 88 at 5700rpm, Weber 32/36DGAV carburettor. 2000GT and S, OHC, bore 90.82mm, stroke 76.95mm, 1993cc (121.6in³), maximum bhp 98 at 5200rpm, Weber 32/36DGV carburettor (note Ford brochures quote 1998cc). 3000GT and Ghia, (V6 OHV) bore 93.66mm, stroke 72.44mm, 2994cc (182.7in³), maximum bhp 138 at 5000rpm, Weber 38/27DGAS carburettor.
GEARBOX: Four-speed, all-synchromesh, floor-mounted gear change. Ratios: 1300, top 4.125, 3rd 5.775, 2nd 8.291, 1st 14.768, reverse 13.695; 1600 top 3.77, 3rd 5.278, 2nd 7.578, 1st 13.497, reverse 12.516; 1600GT and S, top 3.75, 3rd 5.25, 2nd 7.538 1st 13.425, reverse 12.45; 2000 top 3.44, 3rd 4.713, 2nd 6.777,

1st 12.556, reverse 10.870; 3000 top 3.09, 3rd 4.363, 2nd 5.995, 1st 9.764, reverse 10.339.
REAR AXLE: Hypoid bevel, semi-floating. Ratios: 1300 4.125:1; 1600 3.77:1; 1600GT and S 3.75:1; 2000 3.44:1; 3000 3.09:1.
BRAKES: Girling, dual line system, 1300, 1600 and 2000, front 9.625in discs, 1300 rear 8in drums, 1600 and 2000 rear 9in drums, 3000 front 9.75in discs, rear 9in drums, power-assisted on all models except 1300.
STEERING: Rack and pinion, collapsible double-jointed column.
TYRES: 1300, 1600 165 x 13, 2000 175 x 13, 3000 185/70 x 13.
SUSPENSION: Front, MacPherson struts, independent coil springs and anti-roll bar, rear semi-elliptic leaf springs, double telescopic hydraulic shock absorbers, anti-roll bar.
DIMENSIONS: Length with overriders: 14ft 2.9in (4.34m); **width:** 5ft 6.85in (1.698m); **height:** 4ft 3.14in (1.288m); **wheelbase:** 8ft 4.8in (2.559m); **track:** front 4ft 5.3in (1.353m), rear 4ft 6.5in (1.384m); **ground clearance:** 4.1in (10.4cm); **turning circle:** 33ft (10.06m).
APPROXIMATE WEIGHTS: 1300 19cwt 3qtr 15lb (1010kg), 1600S 1ton 1qtr 25lb (1040kg), 2000S 1ton 1qtr 5lb (1031kg), 3000S 1ton 3cwt (1168kg).

CAPACITIES: Fuel 12.7 gallons (57.7 litres). Boot 8.2ft³ (0.23m³), with one rear seat folded down 15.4ft³ (0.432m³), with both rear seats folded down 22.6ft³ (0.634m³).

Ford Capri mark 3

Introduced in March 1978, the mark 3 came with quad headlights, a front spoiler, a simpler front grille, bumpers that wrapped around the sides and larger rear lights incorporating rear fog lights on some models. The front indicators were relocated to the bumper, and most models now had a rear parcel shelf that lifted with the tailgate. Production was discontinued in December 1986. The mark 3 had an unusually long life, remaining substantially unchanged in appearance throughout, with the exception of numerous special editions produced in various colours and with extras such as sunroof and rear spoiler. These specials included, in July 1981, the Cameo based on the L model, and the Calypso, with its two-tone paint scheme based on the LS, then, in May 1982, the Cabaret. The Capri Tickford, produced by Tickford, a division of Aston Martin, was available from 1983. It used a turbocharged version of the 2.8 engine, had many mechanical and cosmetic changes,

and was produced in very limited numbers. The final special edition, the Capri 280, finished in Brooklands Green, appeared in the UK in early 1987. It had 15in wheels instead of the usual 13in.

Mechanical changes to the mark 3 were numerous, and included, from the start, self adjusting brakes, 'see-through' brake fluid reservoirs, retuned carburettors, and gas-filled dampers (not 1300). Other changes were the introduction of viscous-coupled fans, automatic chokes, and all models were fitted with brake fluid warning lights. A five-speed gearbox, initially fitted to the 2.8 Injection model in late 1982, was subsequently adopted for 2000 and 1600 models.

There were the customary equipment upgrades. In August 1978 there was a radio for the L and rear fog lights for the S models. In 1979 there were headlamp washers for Ghia, rear fog lights for the L, and remote door mirrors for GL and S.

The initial range comprised 1300, 1300L, 1600L, 1600GL, 1600S, 2000GL, 2000S, 2000 Ghia, 3000S, 3000 Ghia. In 1981 the 1300 model disappeared, the 1600LS replaced the 1600S, and a 2.8 Injection model replaced the 3000 in July 1981. In 1983 the L, GL, and Ghia ranges were deleted, leaving the 1.6 LS, 2.0S, and 2.8 Injection. Then, in June 1984,

S model identified by graphics along the side.

Calypso model with two-tone paint.

the Laser models appeared. Available with 1.6- and 2.0-litre engines, they replaced the 1.6 LS and 2.0S, and, in September 1984, the 2.8 Injection was replaced by a more fully equipped 2.8 Injection Special, with body-coloured grille and headlight surrounds.

Standard equipment in October 1978 for the 1300 model included a water temperature gauge, heater with two-speed fan, cigarette lighter, lockable glove box with light, two-speed wipers with intermittent wipe, and windscreen washers controlled by a stalk on the steering column, ignition/steering lock, dipping interior mirror, vanity mirror on passenger sun visor, individual front seats with fixed backs, one-piece rear seat, door-operated courtesy light, heated rear window, reversing lights, and power-assisted dual line brakes. L added a radio, reclining front seats, split folding rear seat, colour co-ordinated carpet and fabric-trimmed seats, carpet in load compartment, black rubber bodyside moulding, gas-filled rear shock absorbers. GL added a centre console with clock, handbrake warning light, rear parcel tray, tailgate wash/wipe, rear fog lights, and sports road wheels. S, in addition to GL, featured a trip mileage recorder, tachometer, battery indication meter, oil pressure gauge, integral headrests built into the front seats, sports gear shift knob, black overriders and rear spoiler, 'S' bodyside tape instead of

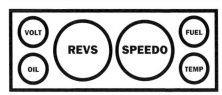

Laser instrumentation.

rubber bodyside moulding, passenger door mirror, alloy road wheels, power steering with 3-litre models. Ghia, in addition to S, added tinted glass, opening rear quarter light, radio/cassette player, rear armrests, grab handle on fascia, centre armrest and storage box, remote control driver's door mirror, tilt/slide sunroof, two-tone horn, rubber bodyside moulding instead of 'S' graphics tape.

Optional extras, according to model, included passenger door mirror, rear wash/wipe, rear parcel tray, headrests, headlight washers, vinyl roof, metallic paint, automatic transmission. Standard equipment for 1986 Laser models, in addition to 'S,' included instrument panel brightness control, tilt/slide sunroof, radio/cassette player with four speakers, tinted glass, centre armrest with storage box, torch key, remote control driver's door mirror, side repeater indicators, body-coloured grille and door mirrors, five-speed gearbox. 2.8 Injection Special, in addition to Laser, featured Recaro sports seats with leather seat surround, opening rear quarter lights, different wheels/tyres.

NUMBER PRODUCED: 324,045 worldwide.
PRICES WHEN INTRODUCED: 1300L £3115, 1600S £4069, 2000GL £4049, 3000S £4594, In 1984 a Laser 2.0 was £6828 and 2.8 Injection Special £9500. By comparison, a Fiesta 950 Popular was £3847, an Escort 1300GL five-door £6097, Granada 2000LX £8162.
COLOURS (1978): Diamond White, Tuscan Beige, Venetian Red, Midnight Blue, Fjord Blue, Highland Green, Black and metallics, Strato Silver, Oyster Gold, Apollo Green, Cosmos Blue, Jupiter Red and Signal Orange, some colours only available on certain models.
COLOURS (1986): Diamond White, Rosso Red, Black and metallics Strato Silver, Crystal Blue, Regency Red, Mercury Grey and two-tones, upper body first, Mercury Grey/Strato Silver, Crystal Blue/Strato Silver.
ENGINE: Four-cylinder in-line engines, 1300, OHV, bore 80.98mm, stroke 62.99mm, 1298cc (79.2in^3), maximum bhp 57 at 5500rpm, Ford GPD 34mm carburettor. 1600, OHC, bore 87.65mm, stroke 66mm, 1593cc (97.2in^3), maximum bhp 72 at 5500rpm, Ford GPD 36mm carburettor. 1600S, maximum bhp 88 at 5700rpm, Weber 32/36DGAV carburettor. 2000S, OHC, bore 90.82mm, stroke 76.95mm, 1993cc (121.6in^3), maximum bhp 98 at 5200rpm, Weber 32/36DGAV carburettor (note Ford brochures quote 1998cc). Six-cylinder V configuration engines, 3000GT and Ghia, OHV, bore 93.66mm, stroke 72.44mm, 2994cc (182.7in^3), maximum bhp 138 at 5100rpm, Weber 38/38EGAS carburettor. 2.8, OHV, bore 93.0mm, stroke 68.5mm, 2792cc (170.4in^3), maximum bhp 160 at 5700rpm, Bosch K-Jetronic fuel-injection.

2.0 Laser.

A 280 (Brooklands) model.

2.8 Injection model.

GEARBOX: Four-speed, all-synchromesh, floor-mounted gear change. Ratios: 1300, top 3.89, 3rd 5.446, 2nd 7.819, 1st 13.926, reverse 12.915; 1600 top 3.77, 3rd 5.278, 2nd 7.578, 1st 13.497, reverse 12.516; S, top 3.75, 3rd 5.25, 2nd 7.538 1st 13.425, reverse 12.45; 2000 top 3.44, 3rd 4.713, 2nd 6.777,

Gear change diagrams: left four-speed, right five-speed.

1st 12.556, reverse 10.870; 3000 and 2.8, top 3.09, 3rd 4.363, 2nd 5.995, 1st 9.764, reverse 10.339. Five-speed, all-synchromesh, 2000 ratios: top 2.855, 4th 3.44, 3rd 4.713, 2nd 6.777, 1st 12.556, reverse 10.870. 2.8 ratios: top 2.549, 4th 3.09, 3rd 3.893, 2nd 5.593, 1st 10.382, reverse 10.413.

REAR AXLE: Hypoid bevel, semi-floating. Ratios: 1300 3.89:1, 1600 3.77:1; 1600S 3.75:1; 2000 3.44:1; 2.8 and 3000 3.09:1; note 2.8 Injection Special has Salisbury limited-slip differential.

BRAKES: Girling, dual line system, 1300 and 1600, front 9.625in discs, 1300 rear 8in drums, 1600 rear 9in drums, 2000S front 9.8in discs, rear 8in drums, 3000 front 9.75in discs, rear 9in drums, 2.8 front 9.76in ventilated discs, rear 9in drums, power-assisted on all models.

STEERING: Rack and pinion, collapsible double-jointed column.

TYRES: 1300, 165 x 13, 1600, 2000 and 3000 185/70 x 13, 2.8 205/60 x 13.

SUSPENSION: Front, MacPherson struts, independent coil springs and anti-roll bar, rear semi-elliptic leaf springs, double telescopic hydraulic shock absorbers, anti-roll bar.

DIMENSIONS: Length: 14ft 4.23in (4.376m); **width**: 5ft 6.85in (1.698m); **height**: 4ft 4.1in (1.323m), 2.8i 4ft 3.1in (1.298m); **wheelbase**: 8ft 4.9in (2.563m); **track**: front 4ft 5.3in (1.353m), rear 4ft 6.5in (1.384m); **ground clearance**: 4.5in (11.51cm); **turning circle**: 35ft 5in (10.8m).

APPROXIMATE WEIGHTS: 1300 19cwt 3qtr 15lb (1010kg), 1600S 1ton 3qtr 2lb (1055kg), 3000S 1ton 3cwt 4lb (1170kg), 2.8i 1ton 4cwt 0qtr, 24lb (1230kg).

CAPACITIES: Fuel 12.7 gallons (57.7 litres). Boot 8.2ft³ (0.23m³), with one rear seat folded down 15.4ft³ (0.432m³), with both rear seats folded down 22.6ft³ (0.634m³).

Capri rear lights: top left mark 1; top right mark 1a; bottom left mark 2; bottom right mark 3. Note how the reversing lights change position: mark 1 has them under the bumper.

Ford Cortina mark 3

Introduced in October 1970 this was an entirely new car. Whereas the mark 2 had used many components from the mark 1, including some of the body structure, the mark 3, with its 'Coke bottle' styling, had an all new floorpan, suspension, steering, engines and more. The boot lid now opened down to bumper level, and the spare wheel was now under the floor, making it easier to fill the boot. Also new was the adoption of L, XL, and GXL titles to replace the previous Deluxe, Super and Executive (E) names. The GT name remained, but gone was the Lotus model. The Capri had been launched with the idea of combining multiple equipment levels and a variety of engines, but with the Cortina available as a two- or four-door saloon and an estate, and a choice of manual or automatic gearbox options, the range exceeded 30 models. Intended to replace both the previous Cortina and the Corsair, the new range extended from the basic 1300 two-door model to the 2000 four-door GXL. With prices ranging from £914 to £1338 there was a Cortina for everyone, from fleet buyers to those that did not perhaps appreciate the styling of the mark 4 Zephyr.

With the Cortina and German-built Taunus

This early L model has been fitted with non-standard alloy wheels.

now using the same basic platform and interior panels, such as the bulkhead and the shared suspension, came the switch to metric for UK cars, the indicator switch also moved from the right- to the left-hand side of the steering column. The new body saw the front quarter lights disappear (they were no longer needed with Aeroflow ventilation system), however the adoption of rectangular vents saw a reduction in effectiveness, and the sloping dashboard, with recessed instruments, also came in for criticism. Problems with lubrication on the new Pinto OHC engines, and various other faults, including some Ford dealerships having to replace rear half-shafts, did not help its reputation either. But despite these, and

Another early L model.

GT model, identified by its twin headlights and black boot trim.

problems with supply, the Cortina quickly became a top selling car in the UK.

As well as rectifying earlier faults, other changes were made to the Cortina during its lifetime, starting with a reduction in the number of models available. September 1973 saw a restyled front end with plastic front grille, with XL models and above featuring rectangular headlights instead of circular units. The new dashboard reverted to the upright style of the mark 2, with the fresh air vents also returning to the mark 2 model's circular style. The only 1600 engine was now the Pinto OHC type, following deletion of the Kent OHV unit. All models now had a front anti-roll bar, and the rear anti-roll bar was revised. There were changes to gearbox ratios for 1300 and 1600 engines, and a new model, the 2000E, was introduced, replacing the GXL. A 2000E estate followed in December 1974.

In October 1975 there were upgrades to lesser models, with all versions now featuring servo-assisted brakes, hazard flashers, driver's door mirror, heated rear window, carpets, and cloth-trimmed seats. All estates except the basic model had tailgate wash/wipe, and L models received rectangular headlights. GT and E models also had some equipment upgrades.

The initial range comprised 1300, 1600, 2000 basic, L, XL saloons and estates, 1600

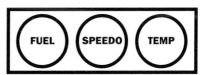

Instrument layout, L models.

and 2000, GT and GXL saloons, with all saloons available as two- or four-door models. Standard equipment for the base model included water temperature gauge, heater/demister/Aeroflow ventilation system, padded fascia, glove box, parcel shelf, two padded sun visors, rubber floor covering, front bucket seats, front-door-operated courtesy lights, two-speed wipers, headlight flasher, foot-operated washer control, combined ignition/steering lock, single horn, and childproof locks on rear doors. L model added height adjustable reclining front seats, carpet instead of rubber floor covering, colour-keyed interior, fully trimmed door panels, three grab handles, coat hooks, cigarette lighter, foot-operated combined windscreen wiper/washer control, reversing lights, rubber inserts in bumpers, and bright metal trim around side windows. XL, in addition to L, featured electric clock, simulated wood interior trim, locking glove box with light, document pocket on driver's sun visor, driver and passenger map pockets, dipping rear view mirror, dual tone horns, hazard warning flashers, bright metal trim around wheelarches, drip rail, waist line, special applique rear panel, and opening rear quarter lights on two-door models. GT, in addition to XL, added tachometer, console unit below dashboard housing oil pressure, water temperature, fuel gauges and ammeter, vanity mirror on passenger sun visor, special front seats with integral headrests, centre console with lift up lid, sports steering wheel and gear knob, four halogen headlight system, coachlines on side panels, no wheelarch mouldings, engine compartment light, power-assisted brakes, sports styled wheels, and anti-roll bar. GXL was generally as GT plus heated rear window, vinyl roof covering, bodyside moulding instead of coachlines, different seats, and rubber faced underriders. By 1976 the XL had gained a tachometer, real wood veneer instrument surround, folding centre armrest, centre

console, vanity mirror, courtesy light operated by all four doors, front seats that reclined enough to create a 'bed,' and driver's door mirror. 2000E was generally as previous GXL, but with single rectangular headlights instead of circular quad headlights.

Cars on this page are GXL models, identified by twin headlights and special boot trim.

Gear change diagram.

The car on this page is an XL model, the above photo showing the rear light arrangement and identification badges.

NUMBER PRODUCED: Total 1,126,559, two-door 143,420, four-door 824,068, estate 154,216 (export only Pick-up 4855).

PRICES AT INTRODUCTION: 1300 Cortina (base model) two-door £914, L four-door £974, L estate £1086, 1600 L four-door £1021, GT four-door £1145, GXL two-door £1259, 2000 XL four-door £1161, GXL four-door £1338, XL estate £1273. Factory-fitted options automatic transmission (not 1300 models) £89, metallic paint £7, vinyl roof £19, radio £35.

COLOURS (1972): Le Mans Green, Sebring Red, Sunset, Monza Blue, Marine Blue, Burgundy Red, Daytona Yellow, Diamond White, Copper Brown and metallics Onyx Green, Evergreen, Tawny, Sapphire Blue, Pearl Grey.

ENGINE: Four-cylinder, 1300 OHV, bore 80.98mm, stroke 62.99mm, 1298cc (79.2in^3), maximum bhp 57 at 5500rpm, Ford 34mm carburettor, 1600 OHV, bore 80.98mm, stroke 77.62mm, 1599cc (97.6in^3), maximum bhp 62 at 5200rpm, Ford 36mm carburettor, 1600 OHC, bore 87.6mm, stroke 66.0mm, 1593cc (97.2in^3), maximum bhp 72 at 5500rpm, Ford 36mm carburettor, 1600GT as 1600 OHC except, maximum bhp 88 at 5700rpm, Weber 32/36DGAV carburettor. 2000 OHC, bore 90.82mm, stroke 76.95mm, 1993cc (121.6in^3), maximum bhp 98 at 5500rpm, Weber 32/36DFAVH carburettor.

GEARBOX: Four-speed, all-synchromesh, floor-mounted gear change. Ratios: 1300 top 4.11, 3rd 5.80, 2nd 9.85, 1st 14.55, reverse 16.29; 1600 OHV and OHC top 3.89, 3rd 5.49, 2nd 9.32, 1st 13.79, reverse 15.41; 1600GT top 3.89, 3rd 5.43, 2nd 7.82, 1st 11.56, reverse 12.93; 2000 top 3.44, 3rd 4.71, 2nd 6.80, 1st 12.56, reverse 12.59. Later cars: 1300 top 4.44, 3rd 6.26, 2nd 10.656, 1st 15.718, reverse 17.584; 1600 OHC top 3.89, 3rd 5.446, 2nd 7.819, 1st 11.553, reverse 12.915; 2000 top 3.75, 3rd 5.138, 2nd 7.388, 1st 13.688, reverse 13.725 (all as per Ford brochures).

REAR AXLE: Hypoid bevel, semi-floating. Ratios: 1300 4.11:1; 1600 OHV and OHC 3.89:1; 2000 3.44:1; later cars 1300 4.44:1; 1600 3.89, 2000 3.75:1.

BRAKES: Girling, front 9.75in discs, rear 8in drums, Pinto OHC engined cars 9in drums, initially power-assisted on 1600GT, 2000 (then all models from October 1975).

STEERING: Rack and pinion, collapsible double-jointed column.

TYRES: 1300 and 1600, 5.60 x 13, 1600GT and 2000 175SR x 13, later 1300, 1600 and 2000 165 x 13, GT 185SR x 13.

SUSPENSION: Front, independent coil springs, double wishbone short and long arms, rear trailing and semi-trailing (upper and lower) radius arms with coil springs, shock absorbers and rubber assist stops, note anti-roll bars were fitted to GT models initially but by 1974 all models had them fitted, front and rear.

DIMENSIONS: Length: 14ft 0in (4.267m); **width:** 5ft 7in (1.703m); **height:** 4ft 4in (1.321m); **wheelbase:** 8ft 5.5in (2.581m); **track:** front and rear 4ft 8in (1.522m); **ground clearance:** 7in (17.8cm); **turning circle:** 32ft (9.7m).

APPROXIMATE WEIGHTS: 1300L 18cwt 2qtr (940kg), 1600XL 18cwt 3qtr 15lb (960kg), 2000E 1ton 20lb (1025kg).

CAPACITIES: Fuel 12 gallons (55 litres). Boot 12ft^3 (0.34m^3), estate 35ft^3 (0.96m^3) or 64ft^3 (1.75m^3) with rear seat folded down.

Ford Taunus models.

Cortina E identified by its special boot trim and 'E' badge on rear pillar. It also retained the twin headlights of the GXL model.

The blue estate is an XL model; the red saloon an L. Both feature the square headlights of later models.

Ford Cortina mark 4

Introduced in September 1976, the mark 4 Cortina returned to its original boxy shape. The curvy lines of Ford's midrange model would not be seen again until the launch of the Sierra, the Cortina's replacement. The mark 4 used the same basic platform as the mark 3, but whereas the mark 3 and Taunus had different body styles, the new body was the same for both Cortina and Taunus models, with only badges to distinguish them. The bonnet was lower than on the mark 3, the front grille was now completely flat, front indicators were no longer on the corners of the wings, the bumpers were of a simpler design, and there was a spoiler incorporated in the valance below the front bumper. At the rear the boot lid no longer opened down to bumper level. A flat panel, like that of the mark 1 and 2 models, and incorporating the rear lights, reappeared. It meant that lifting objects into the boot was now more difficult, but it did make the rear of the car structurally stronger.

L model.

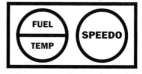

Above: Instrument layout, L models, and below: GL models.

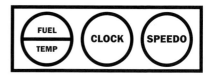

As well as a new body, there were changes to the engine range, with the 1600 now available as an 'economy' unit, as well as in the standard state of tune, with all basic models having the 1300 and 1600 economy engines, but the L model being available with either of the two versions of the 1600 engine. GL models were only available with the standard engine.

There was some restructuring/renaming of the range, with GL replacing the XL, S replacing the GT, and Ghia replacing the 2000E.

Although the lower specification models retained much the same level of equipment as the mark 3 variants, there were some equipment upgrades to other models. In September 1977 a new engine was introduced at the top of the range: the 2.3 V6. It was available with the GL and Ghia saloon and estate and S saloon. Also at this time more Ghia models appeared – a 1600 saloon and estate – and they were fitted with the same engine as used in the Capri 1600S.

The initial range comprised Cortina and L 1300 two- or four-door models, Cortina L and GL 1600 four-door saloons and estates, GL, Ghia 2000 four-door saloons and estates, 2000 S four-door saloon. Standard equipment for the Cortina included water temperature gauge, heating and ventilation system with variable speed fan, cigarette lighter, glove box, two padded sun visors, black carpet, vinyl-trimmed front bucket seats and rear bench seat, front-door-operated courtesy light, front passenger grab handle and two rear coat hooks, childproof locks on rear doors, dipping interior rear view mirror, two-speed wipers, and electrically operated washers controlled by a stalk on the steering column, driver's

GL model.

Crayford convertible.

door mirror, heated rear window, reversing lights, hazard warning lights, chrome bumpers, and boot mat. L added fabric-trimmed seats, reclining front seats, colour-keyed carpet, locking glove box with light, black trinket tray, vanity mirror, two rear grab handles, additional soundproofing, bright trim inserts for windscreens, bright window mouldings and drip rail, bodyside coachline, rubber bumper inserts, opening rear quarter lights on two-door models, and halogen headlights. GL, in addition to L, added a radio, clock, trip mileage recorder, wood instrument surround with black trim, contoured rear seats with centre armrest, door map pockets, sports road wheels, bodyside moulding instead of coachline, and chrome grille surround. S model generally as GL but added tachometer, black console unit with clock, black carpet, Cadiz fabric-trimmed seats with headrests, intermittent wipe facility, black coachline instead of bodyside moulding, black bumpers with rubber inserts and overriders, all-black front grille with twin halogen driving lights, black rear panel, door mirror, handles, window surrounds, etc, uprated suspension with gas-filled shock absorbers. Ghia as GL plus tachometer, velour-trimmed seats with headrests, rear map pockets, fabric door trims with carpeted lower, wood door cappings, front centre armrest, door armrests, rear door courtesy light, boot carpet and light, remote control driver's door mirror, tinted glass, wide bodyside moulding, overriders, wheel rim embellishers on sports wheels, vinyl-covered roof, gas-filled shock absorbers. Estates as saloons, plus rear wash/wipe (except base Cortina). Optional extras, where not fitted as standard, included seatbelts, radio, tinted

GL with the optional Tobacco-coloured vinyl roof.

glass, headlight washers, remote control door mirror, opening sunroof, vinyl roof, and more.

NUMBER PRODUCED: Including mark 5, 1,131,850.

PRICE WHEN INTRODUCED: Cortina 1300 two-door £2045, 1300L four-door £2274, 1600L four-door £2403, 1600GL £2672, 2000GL £2827, 2000 S £3012. Optional extras, alloy road wheels £189, sliding sunroof £132, vinyl roof £72, metallic or Signal paint £28.

COLOURS (1978): Diamond White, Venetian Red, Midnight Blue, Fjord Blue, Highland Green, Sierra Beige and metallics, Strato Silver, Oyster Gold, Apollo Green, Cosmos Blue, Jupiter Red, Roman Bronze. Signal colours, Yellow, Orange.

ENGINE: Four-cylinder, 1300 OHV, bore 80.98mm, stroke 62.99mm, 1298cc (79.2in^3), maximum bhp 50 at 5000rpm, Ford 34mm carburettor. 1600 OHC economy engine, bore 87.6mm, stroke 66.0mm, 1593cc (97.2in^3), maximum bhp 59 at 4500rpm, Ford 36mm carburettor. 1600 standard engine as 1600 OHC economy except, maximum bhp 72 at 5000rpm. 2000 OHC, bore 90.82mm, stroke 76.95mm, 1993cc (121.6in^3), maximum bhp 98 at 5200rpm, Weber 32/36 carburettor. 2.3 (V6 OHV), bore 90mm, stroke 60.14mm, 2294cc (139.98in^3), maximum bhp 108 at 5000rpm, Solex twin-choke 35/35 carburettor.

GEARBOX: Four-speed, all-synchromesh, floor-mounted gear change. Ratios: 1300 top 4.11, 3rd 5.75, 2nd 8.26, 1st 14.71, reverse 13.64; 1600 economy, top 3.78, 3rd 5.29, 2nd 7.60, 1st 13.53, reverse 12.55; 1600 standard, top 3.89, 3rd 5.446, 2nd 7.819, 1st 13.93, reverse 12.915; 2000 top 3.75, 3rd 5.24, 2nd 7.388, 1st 13.688, reverse 13.725; 2300 top 3.444, 3rd 4.72, 2nd 6.78, 1st 12.57, reverse 12.59.

REAR AXLE: Hypoid bevel, semi-floating. Ratios: 1300 4.11:1, 1600 economy 3.78:1, 1600 standard 3.89:1 2000 3.75:1, 2300 3.44:1.

BRAKES: Girling, front 9.75in discs, 1300 and 1600 rear 8in drums, 2000 and 2300 rear 9in drums.

STEERING: Rack and pinion, collapsible double-jointed column, power-assistance standard on 2300, optional on 2000.

Ghia fitted with 'wraparound' bumpers associated with the mark 5 models.

Gear change diagram.

GL estate with period roof rack.

TYRES: 1300 and 1600, 165SR x 13, S and Ghia 185/70SR x 13.

Saloon rear lights: left mark 4; right mark 5.

almost the end of the Cortina name; it was replaced by the radically different designed Sierra in September 1982. The mark 5 was technically similar to the mark 4, with minor modifications to the suspension to improve the ride, and some tweaking of the engines to improve power outputs and increase fuel efficiency, with some cars being fitted

SUSPENSION: Front, independent coil springs, double wishbone short and long arms, rear trailing and semi-trailing (upper and lower) radius arms with coil springs, shock absorbers and rubber assist stops, front and rear anti-roll bars.

DIMENSIONS: **Length**: 14ft 2.3in (4.326m); **width**: 5ft 7in (1.703m); **height**: 4ft 4in (1.321m); **wheelbase**: 8ft 5.5in (2.581m); **track**: front 4ft 8.9in (1.445m), rear 4ft 8in (1.422m); **ground clearance**: 7in (17.8cm); **turning circle**: 32ft 6in (9.8m).

APPROXIMATE WEIGHTS: 1600GL 1ton 0cwt 3qtr (1054kg), 2300S 1ton 2cwt 1qtr (1130kg).

CAPACITIES: Fuel 12 gallons (55 litres). Boot 12ft^3 (0.34m^3), estate 35ft^3 (0.96m^3) or 64ft^3 (1.75m^3) with rear seat folded down.

Ford Cortina 80 (mark 5)

Introduced by Ford in August 1979 as the Cortina 80, it soon became known universally as the Cortina mark 5. This was

Top is an early L model lacking the side trim of higher specification models; middle is an S model; bottom is a 2.3 Ghia with bumper overriders and standard fit vinyl roof.

with new Ford-designed carburettors. The exterior, however, was changed considerably. Larger glass areas were aimed at increasing all round visibility, the front indicators now wrapped around the edges of the front wings, rear lights were larger and now incorporated fog lights, and the plastic end caps of the front and rear bumpers now wrapped around the corners of the wings, extending to the wheelarches. With the door side mouldings, where fitted, being at the same height, this gave the impression that they were an extension of the bumpers. A new front grille that claimed to divert surplus air over the bonnet completed the visual changes.

Modifications that could not be seen were the change to 12-month service intervals from the previous six months, and a new corrosion treatment to improve rust resistance. Inside there were some changes to the fascia, revised seats, and the customary increase in standard equipment. During its short life there were changes to the specification of the various models. In January 1981, the Base model gained fabric trim and the L a passenger door mirror, clock, trip mileage recorder, new seat and door trim. Ghia had a sunroof, and a remote control passenger door mirror.

As was customary with any model that was about to be discontinued there were special editions, both available with two-tone paint

A Ford Taunus.

schemes. The first to appear was the Carousel, in June 1981. Based on the 1300/1600 saloons and estates, but with some GL features, it was followed by the Crusader, available as 1300, 1600 and 2000 saloons and 1600 or 2000 estates in May 1982. Two-tone paint was optional on this model.

The initial range comprised two-door

Above: Ghia; below Carousel special addition.

1300 Base and L saloons, and the following four-door saloons and estates: 1600 Base, L, GL, Ghia and 2000, 2300 GL Ghia. Standard equipment for the Base model included water temperature gauge, heater and ventilation equipment with variable speed fan, glove box, front-door-operated courtesy light, vinyl-trimmed front bucket and rear bench seats, two-speed wipers with flick wipe and electrically operated washers, child proof locks on rear doors, carpet, dipping rear view mirror, black driver's door mirror and bumpers, laminated windscreen, heated rear window, reversing lights, rear fog lights, hazard warning flashers. L added fabric-trimmed seats, vanity mirror, lockable glove box, centre console unit below fascia with radio, cigarette lighter, two-speed wipers with intermittent control, two rear grab handles, Halogen headlights, bright instead of black bumpers/door handles, bodyside tape stripe, opening rear quarter lights on two-door model, estate has wash/wipe. GL in addition to L, had trip mileage recorder, full centre console unit, clock, wood veneer dashboard, door map pockets, front seats with built in 'see-through' headrests, protective bodyside moulding instead of tape stripe, remote control driver's door mirror. Ghia added velour-trimmed seats, radio/cassette player, tachometer, pockets on backs of front seats, carpeted lower sections of door

Ghia 2.0.

trims, wood veneer door cappings, rear-door-operated courtesy light, tinted glass, larger bodyside moulding, overriders, boot carpet and light, and more. Optional extras, where not fitted as standard, included, automatic transmission (not available with 1300 engine), overriders, headlight washers, seats with built-in headrests, remote-controlled door mirrors, passenger door mirror, power steering for 2000 model (standard on 2300).

NUMBER PRODUCED: See mark 4.
PRICE WHEN INTRODUCED: 1300 Base four-door saloon £4003, 1600L £4579, 2000GL £5355, 2300 Ghia £6686.
COLOURS (1980): Diamond White, Venetian Red, Midnight Blue, Corsican Blue, Highland

1.6 L.

Green, Cordoba Beige and metallics, Strato Silver, Solar Gold, Nova Green, Cosmos Blue, Sirius Red, Sable Brown. Signal colours, Yellow, Red.

CAROUSEL COLOURS: Upper body first, Forest Green/Crystal Green, Roman Bronze/Tuscan Beige, Graphite Grey/Strato Silver.

ENGINE: Four-cylinder, 1300 OHV, bore 80.98mm, stroke 62.99mm, 1298cc ($79.2in^3$), maximum bhp 61 at 6000rpm, Ford 34mm VV carburettor. 1600 OHC standard engine, bore 87.6mm, stroke 66.0mm, 1593cc ($97.2in^3$), maximum bhp 75.5 at 5500rpm, Ford 36mm VV carburettor. 1600 Ghia engine as 1600 OHC standard except, maximum bhp 92.5 at 5900rpm, Weber carburettor. 2000 OHC, bore 90.82mm, stroke 76.95mm, 1993cc ($121.6in^3$), maximum bhp 102 at 5400rpm, Weber 32/36 carburettor. 2.3 (V6 OHV), bore 90mm, stroke 60.14mm, 2294cc ($139.98in^3$), maximum bhp 116 at 5500rpm, Solex twin-choke 35/35 carburettor and electronic breakerless ignition.

GEARBOX: Four-speed, all-synchromesh, floor-mounted gear change. Ratios: 1300 top 4.44, 3rd 6.35, 2nd 9.72, 1st 16.25, reverse 18.82; 1600 standard, top 3.78, 3rd 5.29, 2nd 7.60, 1st 13.53, reverse 12.55; 1600 Ghia top 3.89, 3rd 5.33, 2nd 7.66, 1st 14.2, reverse 14.24; 2000 top 3.45, 3rd 4.73, 2nd 6.80, 1st 12.59, reverse 12.62; 2.3 top 3.444, 3rd 4.72, 2nd 6.78, 1st 12.57, reverse 12.59.

REAR AXLE: Hypoid bevel, semi-floating. Ratios: 1300 4.44:1, 1600 standard 3.78:1, 1600 Ghia 3.89:1, 2000 3.45:1, 2300 3.44:1.

Gear change diagram.

Both cars on this page are 1.6 L estates.

BRAKES: Girling, front 9.75in discs, 1300 and 1600 rear 8in drums, 2000 and 2300 rear 9in drums.

STEERING: Rack and pinion, collapsible double-jointed column, power-assisted standard on 2300, optional on 2000.

TYRES: Base, L and GL models 165SR x 13, Ghia 185/70SR x 13.

SUSPENSION: Front, independent coil springs, double wishbone short and long arms, rear trailing and semi-trailing (upper and lower) radius arms with coil springs, gas-filled shock absorbers, front and rear anti-roll bars.

DIMENSIONS: **Length**: saloon 14ft 2.9in (4.341m); **width**: 5ft 7in (1.703m); **height**: 4ft 4in (1.321m); **wheelbase**: 8ft 5.5in (2.581m); **track**: front 4ft 8.9in (1.445m), rear 4ft 8in (1.422m); **ground clearance**: 7in (17.8cm); **turning circle**: 32ft 6in (9.8m). Estate as saloon except **length**: 14ft 6.3 in (4.43m).

APPROXIMATE WEIGHTS: 1600L saloon 1ton 0cwt 1qtr 13lb (1035kg), 1600L estate 1ton 1cwt 3qtr 20lb (1114kg), 2300 Ghia saloon 1ton 1cwt 3qtr 17lb (1113kg), 2300 Ghia estate 1ton 3cwt 1qtr 5lb (1150kg).

CAPACITIES: Fuel 12 gallons (55 litres). Boot 12ft^3 (0.34m^3), estate 34ft^3 (0.96m^3) or 64ft^3 (1.75m^3) with rear seat folded down.

Left, top-to-bottom: Cortina mark 3 GT, later Cortina mark 3, Cortina mark 4.
Right, top-to-bottom: early Cortina mark 3L or XL, later mark 3 Cortina XL, Cortina mark 5.
Note that whereas the Cortina mark 3 had different front grille arrangements for each model, the mark 4 and mark 5 did not.

Ford Granada mark 1 and Consul

Introduced in March 1972 to replace the Zephyr and Zodiac mark 4, the Consul name (previously used for the lowest-engined model of the Zephyr range in 1951) reappeared. Then, just as the original Consul had been renamed the Zephyr in 1962, the new Consul became a Granada in October 1975. The Granada name was new, but the engines were carried over from the Zephyr and Zodiac, albeit uprated, as the Capri engines had been some months earlier. Gearboxes were from the Cortina and Capri, and the inspiration for some other mechanical features, such as rack and pinion steering, also came from the Cortina. The move back to rear drums instead of discs also followed the Cortina and Capri. Almost six inches shorter and one inch narrower than the Zephyr models, the Granada also had a shorter wheelbase, but did feature wider front and rear track. Range revisions during its life included the introduction of estate models in October 1972. The base Granada was renamed XL in early 1974, and a coupé arrived in December 1974. The coupé had been available across Europe since 1972, but this originally had a 'Coke bottle' shaped rear quarter, with the bottom of the glass

following the upward sweep of the body. This was subsequently revised so that, when the UK models arrived, the bottom of the rear quarter glass was in a straight line level with the bottom of the front door window glass. A Ghia saloon model, with new radiator grille and vinyl roof, also appeared in 1974, and there followed a complete revision in 1975 following the deletion of the Consul. Other changes included a 2000 OHC inline four engine replacing the 2000 V4 in September 1974, and general upgrades taking place in 1975, with all models having cloth seat trim, revised Aeroflow vents, heated rear window, hazard flashers, reversing lights, changes to suspension, and more.

A point of note is that standard equipment for all Ford models had increased considerably over the previous 20 years. Items such as heater, water temperature gauge, passenger sun visor, separate front seats instead of bench seats, and windscreen washers were all

Ford Consul L.

Early Granada.

once optional extras, and safety items, such as front and rear seatbelts, childproof locks on rear doors, dual-circuit brake systems and rear fog lights appeared, but gone were steering column gear change with dashboard-mounted handbrake and opening front quarter lights.

In 1976, all Granada production was transferred to Germany. The initial saloon range was Consul 2000 L, 2500 L and 3000 GT, Granada 2500 and 2500 GXL, 3000 and 3000 GXL. The 1976 range was Granada 2000 saloon, 2000 L and 2500 L saloon and estate, 2000 GL and 3000 GL saloon, 3000 GL estate, 3000 S saloon, 2000 Ghia and 3000 Ghia saloon, 3000 Ghia Coupé.

Standard for the Consul were front bucket seats, adjustable for forward or rearward movement only, and a front-door-operated courtesy light. L added rear-door-operated courtesy light, semi-reclining front seats, trip mileage recorder, clock, vanity mirror, map pockets, heated rear window, reversing lights, rubber-faced overriders, and more. Granada, in addition to Consul L, had fully reclining front seats, oil pressure gauge, ammeter, tachometer, centre console, rear compartment heater outlet, wood trim, variable intensity instrument lighting, fog lights, servo-assisted brakes. Granada GXL added a radio with dual speakers, vinyl roof, power-assisted steering, automatic transmission, tinted glass, manually operated sunshine roof, etc.

NUMBER PRODUCED: All UK only production models 123,368 to 1976.

PRICE WHEN INTRODUCED: Consul 2000 L £1428, 2500 L £1539, 3000 GT £1799, Granada 3000 GXL £2299.

COLOURS 1972 Consul: Ermine White, Burgundy Red, Sunset, Electric Blue, Marine Blue, Daytona Yellow, Le Mans Green and metallics, Silver Fox, Fern Green, Evergreen, Sapphire, Pearl Grey, Tawny.

COLOURS 1972 Estates: Diamond White, Sebring Red, Burgundy Red, Sunset, Monza Blue, Marine Blue, Daytona Yellow, Le Mans Green, and metallics, Onyx Green, Evergreen, Sapphire, Pearl Grey, Copper Brown, Tawny.

ENGINE: 2.0 (V4 OHV), bore 93.7mm, stroke 72.4mm, 1996cc (121.8in^3), maximum bhp 81.5 at 5000rpm, Ford GPD carburettor. 2.5 (V6 OHV), bore 93.66mm, stroke 60.35mm, 2495cc (152.2in^3), maximum bhp 120 at 5300rpm, Weber 38/27DGAS carburettor. 3.0 (V6 OHV), bore 93.66mm, stroke 72.41mm, 2995cc (182.76in^3), maximum bhp 138 at 5000rpm, Weber 38/27DGAS carburettor.

Later 2.0 engine four-cylinder in-line, OHC, bore 90.82mm, stroke 76.95mm, 1993cc (121.6in^3), economy engine maximum power 75bhp at 4500rpm, standard engine 99bhp at 5500rpm, Weber carburettor. (Note Ford brochures quote 1998cc for 2.0 OHC engine).
GEARBOX: Four-speed, all-synchromesh, floor-mounted gear change. Ratios: 2.0 top 3.89, 3rd 5.329, 2nd 7.663, 1st 14.199, reverse 14.237; 2.5 top 3.64, 3rd 4.987, 2nd 7.171, 1st 13.286, reverse 13.322; 3.0 top 3.45, 3rd 4.865, 2nd 6.728, 1st 10.902, reverse 11.558.
REAR AXLE: Hypoid bevel, semi-floating. Ratios: 2.0 3.89:1, 2.5 3.64:1, 3.0 3.45:1.
BRAKES: Dual-circuit, power-assisted, front 10.6in discs (ventilated on 3.0), rear 9in drums.
STEERING: Rack and pinion, power-assisted with 3.0 engine, safety steering column with anti-theft steering lock.
TYRES: 2.0 6.45 x 14, 2.5 6.95 x 14, 3.0 175 x 14, Ghia, Consul GT and all estates 185 x 14.
SUSPENSION: Front independent with double wishbone, coil springs and anti-roll bar, rear independent semi-trailing arm/coil spring with plunging constant velocity joints on each half shaft, both front and rear suspension were mounted on sub-frames.
DIMENSIONS: **Length**: saloon 15ft (4.57m); **width**: 5ft 10.5in (1.79m); **height**: 4ft 5.9in

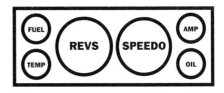

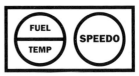

Instrument layout: Granada (top), and Consul.

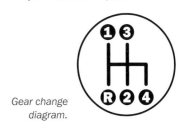

Gear change diagram.

(1.37m); **wheelbase**: 9ft 1in (2.77m); **track**: front 4ft 11.5in (1.51m), rear 5ft 0.6in (1.54m); **ground clearance**: 5.1in (13cm); **turning circle**: 36ft (11m); estate as saloon except **length**: 15ft 4in (4.67m).
APPROXIMATE WEIGHTS: Consul 2.0 L 1ton 1cwt 1qtr 12lb (1086kg), Granada 2.0 GL 1ton 4cwt 3qtr 21lb (1270kg), Granada GXL

Later model Granada Ghia Coupé.

Granada L estate.

saloon 1ton 7cwt 1qtr 21lb (1394kg), GXL
estate 1ton 8cwt 2qtr 15lb (1455kg).
CAPACITIES: Fuel 14.3 gallons (65 litres).
Boot saloon 13.5ft³ (0.38m³), estate 41.7ft³
(1.14m³) or 77ft³ (2.11m³) with rear seat
folded down.

Ford Granada mark 2

Introduced in August 1977 to replace the
mark 1, the only models available were
a saloon and an estate. The body was
restyled, featuring a deep spoiler under the
front bumper, and the new front grille was
squarer and somewhat resembled that of
the Cortina mark 4. The underbody, general
structure, front screen and doors were
based on the superseded Granada mark 1,
as was the rear of the estate model. Inside
there was a new dashboard, and the heating
and ventilation system was modified to suit
the optional air-conditioning. There were
some upgrades to equipment levels, but
broadly they were the same as the original
Granada. There were changes to engine
availability: the 2.0-litre engine remained
but the 2.5- and 3.0-litre units were
replaced with 2.3 and 2.8 units as used
elsewhere in Europe. The 2.8 was available
with a carburettor or fuel-injection, with
the carburettor version being used when

automatic transmission was fitted. There
was a new diesel engine of 2.1 litres for use
in the new Fleet model, replacing the base
model of the range. The Fleet model had an
optional 'Taxi' pack.

In September 1978 GL and Ghia models
gained central locking, and the Ghia model
received electrically operated rear windows
and headlamp washers. The range was also
revised at this time, with GLS models replacing
2.8i S and GL models. A Ghia estate was

An early mark 2 with simpler bumpers.

111

introduced in March 1979, and a 2.3 Ghia saloon in February 1980. In September 1979 and January 1981 there were upholstery upgrades.

Changes for the 1982 model year included new bumpers that wrapped around the corners of the bodywork, a simpler three-bar front grille, fluted rear lights, revisions to suspension, power steering, engines, seats with adjustable lumbar support on GL and Ghia models, and repositioned controls. There were further upgrades in March 1982, with all models having central locking and remote-operated passenger door mirror. A new model was introduced, the Ghia X, with electrically adjustable and heated front seats, air-conditioning, electric sunroof, multi-feature radio/cassette player, and more. Then, in October, the 2.1 diesel engine was replaced by a 2.5 engine. It was available for both saloon and estate models, and came with power steering as standard.

Throughout 1983 there were equipment upgrades and changes to the model range. During the life of the mark 2 there were also a number of special editions produced. In 1979 there was the Sapphire saloon, with two-tone paintwork of Midnight Blue over Strato Silver, based on the 2.8 Ghia. Then, in 1980, there was the Chasseur estate, based on the GL model, with two-tone paintwork

of Roman Bronze and Tuscan Beige, gold-coloured wheels and a roof rack. There was also the Talisman saloon, based on the 2.0 L model with optional 2.3 engine, and available in a range of colours. A further special edition based on the 2.0 L, the Consort, finished in two-tone green appeared in 1981.

The original range comprised 2.1 diesel saloon, 2.0 and 2.3 L saloon and estate, 2.3 GL saloon, 2.8i GL saloon and estate, 2.8i S and Ghia saloons. 2.8 GL and Ghia models were available with automatic transmission. Standard equipment for 1978 L models included radio, clock, fabric-trimmed reclining front seats with headrests, centre console, lockable glove box with light, door pull armrests, two-speed wipers, with intermittent wipe, and washers controlled by a stalk on the steering column, headlight flasher, courtesy lights operated by front and rear doors, heated rear window, reversing lights, hazard warning lights, driver and passenger door mirrors, black bumpers with bright cappings, and black

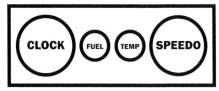

Instrument layout, Granada L.

Early 2.3 L model with simpler bumpers.

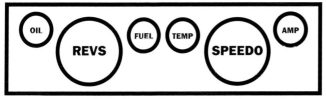 

Instrument layout, Granada 2.8i (left), and gear change diagram.

bodyside moulding. Ghia equipment in addition to L included tachometer, oil pressure gauge, ammeter, simulated wood-trimmed fascia and door cappings, radio/cassette player with front and rear speakers, variable intermittent wipers, crushed velour seat trim, map pockets on the backs of the front seats, two bucket-style rear seats, electrically operated front and rear windows, remote control for driver's door mirror, central door locking, tinted glass, headlight washers, front overriders and rear wraparound mini bumpers, bright insert in bodyside moulding, tilt/slide sunroof, alloy wheels, and more.

NUMBER PRODUCED: 639,440.
PRICE WHEN INTRODUCED: Diesel saloon £4669, 2.0 L estate £4850, 2.3 GL saloon £5261, 2.8i GL saloon £5863, 2.8i S saloon £5910, 2.8i Ghia saloon £6974.
COLOURS 1978: Diamond White, Venetian Red, Midnight Blue, Fjord Blue, Tuscan Beige, Highland Green, and metallics Strato Silver, Jupiter Red, Cosmos Blue, Oyster Gold, Apollo Green.
ENGINE: Four-cylinder OHC, 2.0 bore 90.82mm, stroke 76.95mm, 1993cc (121.6in³), maximum bhp 99 at 5200rpm, Weber carburettor. 2.3 (V6 OHV), bore 90.0mm, stroke 60.1mm, 2293cc (139.9in³), maximum bhp 108 at 5000rpm, Solex carburettor. 2.8 (V6 OHV), bore 93.0mm, stroke 68.5mm, 2792cc (170.4in3), maximum bhp 135 at 5200rpm, Solex carburettor, or 160 at 5700rpm, Bosch K-Jetronic fuel-injection. Diesel engines, four-cylinder OHV, 2.1, bore 90mm, stroke 83mm, 2112cc (129in³), maximum bhp 63 at 4500rpm, Bosch diesel injection. 2.5, bore 94mm, stroke 90mm, 2498cc (152.4in³), maximum bhp 69 at 4200rpm, Roto-Diesel injection.
GEARBOX: Five-speed, all-synchromesh, floor-

mounted gear change. Ratios: 2.0 top 3.17, 4th 3.89, 3rd 5.329, 2nd 7.663, 1st 14.199, reverse 14.237; 2.3 top 2.970, 4th 3.64, 3rd 4.987, 2nd 7.171, 1st 13.286, reverse 13.322; 2.8 top 2.846, 4th 3.45, 3rd 4.865, 2nd 6.728, 1st 10.902, reverse 11.558; 2.5 diesel saloon, top 2.97, 4th 3.64, 3rd 5.096, 2nd 8.44, 1st 14.232, reverse 13.322. Four-speed gearbox ratios as 1st to 4th of five-speed gearbox. 2.1 diesel, 4th 3.89, 3rd 5.524, 2nd 9.064, 1st 15.404.
REAR AXLE: Hypoid bevel, semi-floating. R: petrol cars 2.0 3.89:1, 2.3 3.64:1, 2.8 3.45:1; diesel cars 2.1 3.89:1, 2.5 saloon 3.64:1, estate 3.89:1.
BRAKES: Dual-circuit, power-assisted, front 10.3in discs (ventilated on 2.8), rear 9in drums.
STEERING: Rack and pinion, power-assisted with 2.8 engine, safety steering column with anti-theft steering lock.
TYRES: Saloons 2.0, 2.3, 2.1, 175 x 14, 2.8, 185 x 14, 2.8i, 195/60 x 14, estates 2.0, 2.3, 2.8, 185 x 14, 2.8i, 195/60 x 14.
SUSPENSION: Front independent with double wishbone, coil springs and anti-roll bar, rear independent semi-trailing arm/coil spring with plunging constant velocity joints on each half shaft.
DIMENSIONS: Length: saloon 15ft 2.28in (4.63m); **width:** 5ft 10.5in (1.79m); **height:**

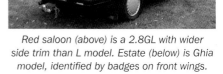

Red saloon (above) is a 2.8GL with wider side trim than L model. Estate (below) is Ghia model, identified by badges on front wings.

Gear change diagram.

4ft 5.9in (1.37m); **wheelbase**: 9ft 1in (2.77m); **track**: front 4ft 11.5in (1.51m), rear 5ft 0.6in (1.54m); **ground clearance**: 5.1in (13cm); **turning circle**: 34.4ft (10.5m); estate as saloon except **length**: 15ft 7.4in (4.76m).
APPROXIMATE WEIGHTS: 2.0 L 1ton 4cwt 1qtr 19lb (1240kg), 2.3 GL 1ton 6cwt 0qtr 20lb (1330kg), 2.8i 1ton 6cwt 2qtr 1lb (1350kg), 2.1 diesel 1ton 6cwt 0qtr 23lb (1332kg).
CAPACITIES: Fuel 14.3 gallons (66 litres). Boot saloon 14.3ft^3 (0.39m^3), estate 41.7ft^3 (1.14m^3) or 77ft^3 (2.11m^3) with rear seat folded down.

Ford Granada mark 3

Introduced in April 1985, this was an entirely new car. A large hatchback initially, replacing both the saloon and estate car models of the previous Granada, a saloon model followed in January 1990, and an estate in March 1992. The introduction of the Granada's replacement, the Scorpio, in January 1995, would see the disappearance of the hatchback and the return to saloon and estate models of Ford's largest car. With its completely redesigned body, the Granada now featured large polycarbonate bumpers designed to absorb impacts and provide protection to the metal bodywork behind them. This type of bumper had been introduced with the Sierra, and would soon become standard for all Fords, as well as other manufacturers. The Granada also featured Sierra-style front and rear suspension, but was the first Ford to be fitted with an anti-lock braking system (ABS) as standard equipment, and also the first without guttering so roof racks could no longer be attached. Eventually, estate cars would feature longitudinal bars attached permanently to the roof, which could then have transverse bars fitted to them to construct a roof rack. Along with the lack of guttering came flush-fitting glass. This extended back towards the tailgate, with no large metal quarter panels to obstruct rear vision. Other new features were a lockable fuel filler cap, high security door locks developed by Chubb, a name synonymous with locks and security systems, and the radio aerial was incorporated into the rear window heating element.

Changes during its lifetime included revisions to engine availability. The first diesel engines introduced in April 1986 were from Peugeot. These were replaced in November 1988 with turbo-charged Peugeot units, then, in September 1993, Ford turned to the Italian VM company for its diesel engines. There were also the usual changes to model range and upgrades to specifications. These included the introduction of 4x4 versions of the 2.8i Ghia and Scorpio models in October 1985, with the power split 34/66 between front and rear wheels, and the introduction of an L model in 1986. Then, in 1987, the 2.4 engine appeared, and the 2.8 engine was replaced with a 2.9 unit. Also at this time the Ghia X was introduced. Ghia models were fitted with headlight wash/wipe and fog lights, and L and GL models gained power-assisted steering. June 1989 saw a new 2.0 double overhead cam engine replace the earlier 2.0 single overhead cam unit, and the L model was replaced by the LX. All models received anti-theft alarms, and Ghia, Ghia X gained heated front windscreens.

In 1990, when the saloon was introduced, there were changes to suspension settings, a new front grille, and all models were fitted with

Above and overleaf: Ghia model identified by cladding on the lower side of the car.

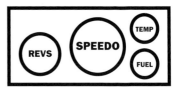

Instrument layout, Granada (1990).

body-coloured bumpers. Then, in April 1991, a Cosworth-developed 24-valve version of the 2.9 V6 engine was introduced for Scorpio models. It was fitted with full electronic ignition and a catalytic converter. In 1992, with the introduction of the estate, came revisions to front end styling, with new bonnet, wings, grille and headlights with the indicator lenses now being white. In September 1993 all models were fitted with a driver's airbag.

The initial range comprised 1.8, 2.0 GL, 2.0i GL and Ghia, 2.8i Ghia and Scorpio, six hatchbacks only. By 1993 the range had increased to become 2.0i LX, GLX, Executive, Ghia, Scorpio, 2.9i GLX, Executive, Ghia, Scorpio, 2.5 diesel Ghia, Executive, Scorpio hatchbacks, saloons and estates; thirty-six models excluding the various automatic options. The 2.4i models were only produced for a short time, from 1987 to 1989.

Standard equipment for 1986 GL included radio/cassette player, centre console, dimmable instrument lighting, variable speed wipers, front seat headrests, reclining height adjustable front seats, split folding rear seat, inertia reel front seatbelts, steering column adjustable for rake and reach, courtesy lights operated by all doors, driver and passenger door mirrors, and bodyside moulding. Ghia added tachometer, overhead console, digital clock with multi-function information display, rear seat headrests, map pockets in back of front seats, electrically operated front and rear windows, electrically operated and heated door mirrors, sunroof, and bright window trim. Scorpio, in addition to Ghia, added air-conditioning, courtesy lights with delayed switch-off,reading and front and rear footwell lights, electrically operated sunroof, heated front windscreen, cladding to lower bodyside instead of strip moulding, headlight washers, integrated auxiliary front driving lights, etc.

PRICE WHEN INTRODUCED: 1.8 GL £8514, 2.0 GL £8877, 2.0i GL £9276, 2.8i GL £11,678, 2.8i Scorpio £15,550, 2.8i Scorpio 4 x 4 £18,100.

COLOURS 1986: Diamond White, Ivory, Lacquer Red, Ocean Blue, and metallics Strato Silver, Nimbus Grey, Quartz Gold, Silver Sage, Chestnut, Regency Red, Paris Blue, Mineral Blue, Raven.

ENGINE (1985): Four-cylinder, OHC, 1.8 bore 86.2mm, stroke 79.65mm, 1796cc (109.6in^3), maximum bhp 88.5 at 5400rpm, Pierburg 2V carburettor. 2.0, bore 90.82mm, stroke 76.95mm, 1993cc (121.6in^3), maximum bhp 99 at 5200rpm, Weber carburettor or 113 at 5200rpm, Bosch L-Jetronic fuel-injection. 2.8 (V6 OHV), bore 93.0mm, stroke 68.5mm, 2792cc (170.4in^3), maximum bhp 148.2 at 5800rpm, Bosch L-Jetronic fuel-injection. Peugeot diesel engine, four-cylinder, bore 94mm, stroke 90mm, 2498cc (152.4in^3), maximum bhp 68.4 at 4500rpm, Bosch EP/VAC injection.

ENGINE (1987 onwards): Six-cylinder, V formation, DOHC, 2.4, bore 84mm, stroke 72mm, 2394cc (146.06in^3), maximum bhp 125 at 5800rpm, Bosch LE-Jetronic fuel-injection. 2.9 bore 93mm, stroke 71.99mm, 2935cm (179in^3), maximum bhp 191.8 at 5750rpm, Bosch LH-Jetronic fuel-injection. 2.9 OHC, as 2.9 DOHC except two valves per cylinder instead of four, maximum bhp 145

at 5500rpm, Bosch LE-jetronic fuel-injection. Note some engines were fitted with catalytic converters which reduced maximum bhp. VM diesel, four-cylinder, bore 92mm, stroke 94mm, 2500cc (152.5in^3), maximum bhp 115 at 4200rpm, Bosch injection system with Garrett turbocharger. 2.0 four-cylinder DOHC, bore 86mm, stroke 86mm, 1998cc (121.9in^3), maximum bhp 118 at 5500rpm, Ford electronic ignition and fuel-injection system.

Gear change diagram.

Late Granada mark 3 models with revised bonnet, front wings and lights.

GEARBOX: Five-speed, all-synchromesh, floor-mounted gear change. Ratios: 2.0 top 3.21, 4th 3.92, 3rd 5.253, 2nd 8.154, 1st 15.249, reverse 13.759. 2.4 top 3.018, 4th 4.038, 3rd 5.684, 2nd 8.389, 1st 13.406, reverse 14.19. 2.5 diesel top 2.706, 4th 2.957, 3rd 4.434, 2nd 6.989, 1st 11.769, reverse 10.628. 2.9 four-speed automatic, top 2.73, 3rd 3.64, 2nd 5.351, 1st 8.991, reverse 7.68. All above based on axle ratios below.

REAR AXLE: Hypoid bevel, semi-floating. Ratios: petrol cars 2.0 and 2.4 3.92:1, 2.8 3.36:1, 2.9 automatic 3.64:1, 2.9 4x4 3.62:1; diesel cars 3.36, note optional alternative ratios were available for many models.

BRAKES: Dual-circuit, power-assisted, with electronic ABS, front 10.2in ventilated discs, rear 9.96in discs. Scorpio 24v, front 10.9in discs, rear 10.75in discs.

STEERING: Rack and pinion, (power-assisted on 2.8i), safety steering column with anti-theft steering lock.

TYRES: 1.8 and 2.0, 175 x 14, 2.0i and 2.8i 185/70 x 14, later cars all 185/70 x 14 except Ghia X and Scorpio 195/65 x 15.

SUSPENSION: Front, MacPherson struts, offset coil sprung twin-tube telescopic shock absorbers, anti-roll bar, rear with progressive rate coil springs, semi-trailing arms, telescopic shock absorbers, anti-roll bar, self levelling suspension optional with some models.

DIMENSIONS: **Length**: hatchback 15ft 3.9in (4.67m); **width**: 5ft 9.3in (1.76m); **height** 4ft 8.7in (1.44m); **wheelbase**: 9ft 0.7in (2.76m); **track**: front and rear 4ft 10.1in (1.475m); **ground clearance**: 4.7in (12cm); **turning circle**: 36ft 1.2in (11m), saloon and estate as hatchback except **length**: 15ft 6.8in (4.745m).

APPROXIMATE WEIGHTS: hatchbacks, 1.8 GL 1ton 3cwt 1qtr (1180kg), 2.0 GL 1ton 3cwt 1qtr 9lb (1185kg), 2.8 Ghia 1ton 6cwt 2qtr 9lb (1350kg), 2.4 Ghia 1ton 5cwt 2qtr (1295kg), 2.9 Ghia 1ton 6cwt 0qtr 3lb (1322kg), 2.9 Scorpio 1ton 6cwt 3qtr 7lb (1362kg).

CAPACITIES: Fuel 15.4 gallons (70 litres). Boot saloon 17.3ft^3 (0.49m^3), hatchback 15.5ft^3 (0.439m^3) or 47.7ft^3 (1.35m^3) with rear seat folded down.

Ford Scorpio (1995)

Introduced in January 1995, the new Scorpio saw a return to saloon and estate

models only of Ford's largest car. It was discontinued in 1998. All cars had gradually increased in size over the years, and the 1982 Sierra was larger than the original large Ford car of the 1950s, the Zephyr. By 2008 the Mondeo had overtaken the Scorpio in size. With its completely redesigned front and rear the Scorpio provoked the same mixed reactions the Sierra had when it replaced the Cortina. But there were hidden improvements over the Granada. Many new safety features came as standard, such as side impact bars in the doors, a feature of the 1993 Probe, and driver's airbag (a passenger airbag was optional). The estate cars featured longitudinal bars attached permanently to the roof, and rubbing strips on the flat section of the roof behind the sunroof to protect the paintwork; thus a roof rack could be created.

Changes during its lifetime included the introduction of a 2.3 petrol engine in April 1996, at which time the range was revised with the deletion of the Executive model and the introduction of a Ghia X. There were also styling changes in January 1998. The initial range was reduced in comparison with the Granada it replaced, and comprised Executive

saloon or estate models with 2.0 engines with 8 or 16 valves, 2.9 engines with 12 or 24 valves, and a 2.5 diesel engine. There were also Ghia and Ultima versions of all the Executive models except the 8-valve 2.0 engine. Standard equipment for the Executive included, tachometer, digital total mileage and trip recorder, stereo radio/cassette player, front door bins, front- and rear-door-operated courtesy lights, rear compartment heating ducts, reach and rake adjustable steering column, fully reclining front seats with adjustable headrests and electrical height adjustment for the driver's seat, 60/40 split rear seat with folding centre armrest and headrests, storage pockets in rear of front seats, centre console with cassette storage, illuminated glove box with lid, tilt/slide sunroof with louvered blind, carpeted luggage compartment, alarm, manual adjustment of door mirrors. Ghia added, multi-function information display module, delayed switch-off courtesy lights, centre console storage box with lid, electrically operated sunroof, electrically operated and heated door mirrors, and 'Quickclear' heated windscreen. Ultima added CD autochanger, footwell and door marker/kerbside courtesy lights, electrical ten-function adjustable driver's seat with

personalised memory, leather-trimmed seats, air-conditioning, cruise control, front fog lights, and more.

PRICE WHEN INTRODUCED: Saloons: Executive 2.0i 8v £16,600, Executive 2.9 12v automatic £18,185, Ultima 2.9 12v automatic £20,720; estates: Executive 2.0i 8v £17,110, Ghia 2.9 24v automatic £25,405.

COLOURS (1995): Ontario Blue, Dark Maroon and metallics, Auralis Blue, Dark Aubergine, Nantucket Grey, Ash Black, Tourmallard, Petrol Blue, State Blue, Loden Green, Nouveau Red.

ENGINE: All petrol engines have fuel-injection and EEC engine management system with electronic breakerless ignition. Four-cylinder, 2.0 bore 86mm, stroke 86mm, 1998cc (121.9in^3), OHC 8v, maximum bhp 115 at 5500rpm, DOHC 16v, 136 at 6300rpm. 2.3 DOHC 16v bore 89.6mm, stroke 91mm, 2295cc (140in^3),

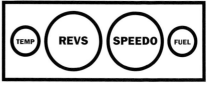

Instrument layout.

maximum bhp 147 at 5600rpm. 2.9 V6, bore 93mm, stroke 72mm, 2935cc (179in^3), OHC 12v, maximum bhp 150 at 5500rpm. DOHC 24v, 207 at 6000rpm. 2.5 diesel, four-cylinder, bore 92mm, stroke 94mm, 2500cc (152.5in^3), maximum bhp 115 at 4200rpm.

GEARBOX: Five-speed, all-synchromesh, floor-mounted gear change. Ratios: 2.0 8v, top 3.354, 4th 4.09, 3rd 5.481, 2nd 8.507, 1st 15.91, reverse 14.356; 2.0 16v, top 3.501, 4th 4.27, 3rd 5.807, 2nd 8.882, 1st 15.415, reverse 13.92; 2.3 16v, top 3.206, 4th 3.91, 3rd 5.630, 2nd 8.133, 1st 14.115, reverse 12.747; 2.5 TD, top 2.554, 4th 3.36, 3rd 4.569, 2nd 6.989, 1st 12.129, reverse 10.954; four-speed automatics, 2.0 8v, top 2.94, 3rd 3.92, 2nd 5.762, 1st 9.682, reverse 8.27; 2.0 16v, top 3.203, 3rd 4.27, 2nd 6.277, 1st 10.547, reverse 9.01; 2.9 12v and 24v, top 2.73, 3rd 3.64, 2nd 5.351, 1st 8.991, reverse 7.68.

REAR AXLE: Ratios manual, 2.0 8v 4.09:1, 2.0 16v 4.27:1, 2.3 16v 3.92:1, 2.5 3.36:1, automatics, 2.0 8v 3.92:1 or 4.09:1, 2.0 16v 4.27:1, 2.3 16v 3.92:1, 2.9 3.64:1

BRAKES: Power-assisted with separate hydraulic circuits for front and rear brakes and electronic anti-lock system, front 10.2in ventilated discs, rear 10in solid rear discs (ventilated with estate and 24v models).
STEERING: Rack and pinion, power-assisted (speed sensitive on V6 models).
TYRES: Executive 195/65 x 15, Ghia and Ultima 215/60 x 15, all 24v models 225/50ZR x 16.
SUSPENSION: Front, MacPherson strut, gas-filled shock absorbers, forged 'A' arm with horizontal bushes and integral fluid damping, rear semi-trailing arms and anti-roll bar with progressive rate coil springs, shock absorbers and suspension arm mountings on subframe. Rear suspension self levelling on estate models.
DIMENSIONS: Length: saloon 15ft 9.99in

(4.825m), **width**: without mirrors 5ft 9.3in (1.76m), with mirrors 6ft 1.8in (1.875m); **height**: 4ft 6.6in (1.388m); **wheelbase**: 9ft 1in (2.77m); **track**: front 4ft 10.3in (1.48m), rear 4ft 10.9in (1.495m); **ground clearance**: 4.7in (12cm); **turning circle**: 34ft (10.4m), estate as saloon except **length**: 15ft 10in (4.826m), height 4ft 8.77in (1.442m).
APPROXIMATE WEIGHTS: saloons, Executive 2.0i 8v 1 ton 8cwt 3qtr 21lb (1470kg), Ghia 2.0i 16v 1ton 9cwt 11lb (1478kg), Ultima 2.9i 24v 1ton 12cwt 1qtr (1638kg), weight estates, Executive 2.0i 8v 1ton 9cwt 3qtr (1511kg), Ultima 2.9 24v 1ton 12cwt 3qtr 16lb (1671kg).
CAPACITIES: Fuel 15.4 gallons (70 litres). Boot saloon 16.4ft^3 (0.465m^3), estate 19.4ft^3 (0.55m^3) or 56.5ft^3 (1.6m^3) with rear seat folded down.

Gear change layout.

Ford Fiesta mark 1

Launched in Britain in February 1977, the Fiesta, codenamed Bobcat, was Ford's first front-wheel drive car, and was intended to fill the gap in the 'supermini' class, dominated by the likes of the Renault 5 and Volkswagen Polo. It followed the same format as these cars, being a 'hatchback': a defining term that has since come to be included in dictionaries along with saloon and coupé. For its new range Ford needed new engines to fit transversally at the front. This allowed the car to retain the same passenger space as a rear-wheel drive model, whilst reducing the overall length and eliminating the need for a transmission tunnel running through the interior. Modified MacPherson strut suspension fitted with tie bars, bulkhead-mounted steering with a decoupling joint designed to break in the event of a major impact, plus dual-circuit brakes split diagonally (ie O/S front and N/S rear rather than a system with separate circuits for the front and the rear, were all new features introduced for the Fiesta.

The new engine (based on the Kent powerplant used in other Ford models) had a three-bearing crankshaft. Ford's engines had moved to five-bearing crankshafts in the 1960s, but, in order to fit the engine transversally, it was necessary to keep it shorter. Initially, two engines were available: 957cc and 1117cc. A 1298cc engine joined the range in September 1977, based on the unit used in some Escort models. It had a five-bearing crankshaft but was modified to fit transversally. Following the introduction of this 1298cc engine changes were made to the suspension of those models fitted with it. Other changes were made in September 1978, at which point L and S models were fitted with a rear wash/wipe, and some models received radios. In October 1978, the first of the special editions, the Kingfisher, appeared. It was available with Cosmos Blue/Strato Silver two-tone paint, and came with sunroof, headrests and remote control driver's door mirror. In April 1979, special valves were fitted to the brakes to prevent the rear wheels locking up under harsh braking. In September 1979, there were

Fiesta L.

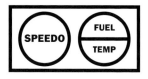

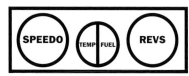

Instrument diagrams: L model (top) and S and Ghia.

equipment upgrades to some models, and another special edition: the Sandpiper. After this came the Firefly, Supersport, and Festival.

In December 1980, the base models were replaced with the Popular 950 and Popular Plus 1100. Early 1981 saw more special editions – the Sandpiper 2 and Bravo – then, in September, the XR2 was introduced, with a 1597cc engine. There were further equipment upgrades, suspension changes, electronic

Fiesta XR2.

ignition for 1300 and 1600 engines, and larger section bumpers.

In 1983 further special editions were released – the Quartz and Finesse – just ahead of the launch of the Fiesta mark 2.

The initial mark 1 range comprised 950 Base, L, Ghia, 1100 L, S and Ghia. Standard equipment included vinyl-covered front bucket seats with anti-tip lock, folding rear bench seat, static seatbelts, two-speed wipers with flick wipe, foot-operated windscreen washers, driver's side storage compartment, passenger side glove compartment, and parcel shelf. L model added fabric-covered five-position reclining front seats, inertia reel instead of static seatbelts, dipping rear view mirror, driver's door mirror, driver and passenger door storage bins, front and rear armrests, folding rear parcel shelf, heated rear window, halogen headlights, reversing light, and bright side trim strip. S, in addition to L, added a tachometer, mileage trip recorder, intermittent wipe instead of flick wipe facility, electrically operated windscreen washers, cigarette lighter, centre console with clock, illuminated glove box with lid, detachable rear parcel shelf, bodyside coachline instead of bright strip. Ghia, in addition to S, had velour-trimmed seats, map pockets, mahogany effect instrument binnacle,

centre console and heater panel, vanity mirror, radio, rear screen wash/wipe, bright bumpers with vinyl inserts and overriders, bodyside protection moulding, and more.

NUMBER PRODUCED: UK 307,600.
PRICE IN JULY 1977: 950, Base £2114, L £2329, Ghia £2969, 1100, L £2443, Ghia £3083, S £2680.
COLOURS (1977): Diamond White, Peppermint Green, Royal Blue, Bermuda Blue, Nevada Beige, Venetian Red, Signal Yellow, Signal Amber and metallics, Strato Silver, Hawaiian Blue, Jupiter Red, Regency Green, Oyster Gold, Roman Bronze.
ENGINE (1980): Four-cylinder, OHV, 950, bore 74mm, stroke 55.7mm, 957cc (58.4in³), maximum bhp Base model 40 at 5500rpm; L and GL 45bhp at 6000, Ford sonic idle carburettor; 1100, bore 74mm, stroke 65mm, 1117cc (68.16in³), maximum bhp 55 at 5700rpm, Ford sonic idle carburettor; 1300, bore 81mm, stroke 63mm, 1298cc (79.2in³), maximum bhp 66 at 5600rpm, Ford twin-barrel downdraft carburettor.
GEARBOX (1980): Four-speed, all-synchromesh, floor-mounted gear change. Ratios: 950 Base and all 1100 models, top 3.89, 3rd 5.459, 2nd 8.315, 1st 14.533,

Fiesta 1.3.

Gear change diagram.

reverse 15.287; 950 L, GL, top 4.114, 3rd 5.774, 2nd 8.795 1st 15.371, reverse 16.169; 1300, top 3.684, 3rd 5.171, 2nd 7.876, 1st 13.766, reverse 14.48. Front-wheel drive, final drive ratio 950 Base and all 1100 models, 4.056:1, 950 L, GL 4.29:1, 1300 3.842:1.
BRAKES: Dual-circuit with pressure limiting valve, front 8.71in discs, rear 7.0in drums, power-assisted on 1100 and 1300 models.
STEERING: Rack and pinion.
TYRES: Base model 135SR x 12, other models 145SR x 12.
SUSPENSION: Front MacPherson struts, coil springs, telescopic shock absorbers, rear 5 bar link with trailing arms, coil springs, telescopic shock absorbers and solid axle with Panhard rod.
DIMENSIONS: **Length**: 11ft 8.4in (3.565m); **width**: 5ft 1.7in (1.567m); **height**: 4ft 3.7in (1.314m); **wheelbase**: 7ft 6in (2.286m); **track**: front 4ft 4.5in (1.334m), rear 4ft 4in (1.321m); **ground clearance**: 5.51in (14cm); **turning circle**: 31ft (9.45m).
APPROXIMATE WEIGHTS: 950 L 14cwt 6lb (714kg), 1100 S 14cwt 26lb (723kg), 1100 Ghia 14cwt 1qtr 7lb (727kg).
CAPACITIES: Fuel 7.5 gallons (34 litres). Boot 7.1 ft3 (0.2m³), or 42.6ft³ (1.205m³) with rear seat folded down.

Ford Fiesta mark 2

Introduced in August 1983, as well as changes to the front and rear styling, with lower bonnet line and rear light cluster now including the reversing lights instead of them being under the rear bumper, there were many mechanical improvements. A five-speed gearbox became optional on 1100, it was standard for the 1300 and 1600 engines both of which were now the CVH (Compound Valve angle Hemispherical combustion chamber) type, as fitted from 1980 to the Escort mark 3. There was also a diesel engine available for the Popular Plus and L models, and, of course, there were the usual equipment upgrades all round. Changes in 1984 included revised shape headrests, and models with 950 engines were fitted with power-assisted brakes. In 1986, the 1300 engine was replaced by a 1400, electronic ignition was fitted to 950 and 1100 engines, and all models received the 8.8-gallon fuel tank that had previously only been fitted to the XR2. There were also special editions: Finesse II, Holiday and Firefly, plus a new model, the 1.4S. More special editions were introduced in 1987, and CTX (Continuously variable TransaXle) automatic transmission became available with the 1100 engine.

The initial model range comprised 950 Popular, Popular Plus, L, 1100 Popular Plus, L, Ghia, 1300 L, Ghia and 1600 diesel Popular Plus and L models. The XR2 followed shortly after. Gone were the GL and S models that had been part of the Fiesta mark 1 range. Unlike its predecessor, the new XR2 had the same headlights and indicators as other

Above and opposite: Ghia model, identified by wide bodyside moulding.

models in the range, as opposed to having completely different front end styling, but to differentiate it from lesser models the new XR2 had large black skirts under the bumpers. These skirts joined up with the wheelarch extensions, which, in turn, were joined by sill extensions, A red pinstripe along the side replaced the earlier XR2 graphics, and the rear spoiler was replaced by strips across the top and down the sides of the rear window.

Standard equipment for all models included fabric-trimmed reclining front bucket seats with anti-tip lock, folding rear bench seat, front inertia reel seatbelts, two-speed wipers with flick wipe, electric windscreen washers, two-speed heater fan, driver and passenger parcel shelves, stowage bins in front doors, grey painted steel bumpers, driver's door mirror, anti-dazzle rear view mirror, reversing lights, rear foglight, and hazard warning flashers. L model added radio, clock, centre console, cigarette lighter, 60/40 split rear folding seat, passenger door mirror, remote control of driver's door mirror, dipping rear view mirror, headrests on front seats, removable rear parcel shelf, heated rear window, tailgate wash/wipe, halogen headlights, lockable fuel cap, grey bodyside moulding. Ghia, in addition to L, had radio/cassette player with speaker balance control, tachometer, trip mileage recorder, intermittent instead of flick wipe front windscreen wipers, three-speed heater fan, glove box instead of

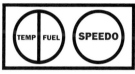

Instrument diagram, Popular, Popular Plus, L models.

passenger parcel shelf, velour-trimmed seats, cloth door inserts, vanity mirror on passenger sun visor, tinted glass, grey plastic bumpers with inserts and overriders, wide bodyside protection moulding with insert, bright instead of body-coloured window surrounds, electric tailgate release, sunroof, and more. XR2 equipment generally as Ghia but with fabric-trimmed seats, sports steering wheel, black window surrounds, additional bodywork mouldings, and unique styled steel wheels.

PRICE IN 1984: 950 Popular £3701, L £4491, 1100 L £4890, 1300 Ghia £5731. **COLOURS (1984)**: Diamond White, Coral Beige, Rio Brown, Sunburst Red, Cardinal Red, Ocean Blue, Ceramic Blue, and metallics Strato Silver, Champagne Gold, Jade Green, Imperial Red, Glacier Blue, Caspian Blue. XR2 only colours available Diamond White, Sunburst Red or optional Black. **ENGINE (1984)**: Four-cylinder, 950 OHV, bore 74mm, stroke 55.7mm, 957cc (58.4in³), maximum bhp 45 at 5700, Ford VV carburettor. 1100 OHV, bore 74mm, stroke

Four- and five-speed gear change diagrams.

65mm, 1117cc (68.2in^3), maximum bhp 50 at 5000rpm, Ford VV carburettor. 1300 OHC, bore 79.96mm, stroke 64.52mm, 1296cc (79.1in^3), maximum bhp 69 at 6000rpm, Ford VV downdraft carburettor. 1600 OHC, bore 79.96mm, stroke 79.52mm, 1598cc (97.5in^3), maximum bhp 96 at 6000rpm, Weber 32/34 DFT carburettor. Diesel OHV, bore 80mm, stroke 80mm, 1608cc (98.1in^3), maximum bhp 54 at 4800rpm.

GEARBOX (1984): Four-speed, all-synchromesh, floor-mounted gear change. Ratios: 950, top 3.857, 3rd 5.459, 2nd 8.286, 1st 14.533, reverse 15.287. 1100, top 3.146, 3rd 4.644, 2nd 7.32 1st 12.838, reverse 13.504. Five-speed, all-synchromesh, ratios: 1100 and 1300, top 2.905, 4th 3.654, 3rd 5.171, 2nd 7.849, 1st 13.766, reverse 13.889; 1600, top 2.709, 4th 3.407, 3rd 4.568, 2nd 6.854, 1st 11.301, reverse 12.953; diesel

top 2.52, 4th 3.17, 3rd 4.25, 2nd 6.376, 1st 11.942, reverse 12.049. Front-wheel drive, final drive ratio: 950 4.056:1, 1100 3.583:1, 1100 with five-speed gearbox and 1300 3.842:1, 1600 3.583:1, diesel 3.333:1.

BRAKES: Dual-circuit with pressure limiting valve, front 8.71in discs, rear 7.0in drums, XR2 front 9.4in discs, power-assisted on 1100, 1300, 1600 models.

STEERING: Rack and pinion.

TYRES: 950 and 1100, 135SR x 12, 1300 155/70SR x 12, 1600 185/60 x 13.

SUSPENSION: Front MacPherson struts, coil springs and telescopic shock absorbers, rear, trailing arms, coil springs, telescopic shock absorbers and solid beam axle with Panhard rod.

DIMENSIONS: Length: 11ft 11.7in (3.65m); **width:** 5ft 2.4in (1.58m); **height:** 4ft 4.2in (1.33m); **wheelbase:** 7ft 6in (2.286m); **track:** front 4ft 5.82in (1.37m), rear 4ft 3.97in

(1.32m); **ground clearance**: 5.51in (14cm); **turning circle**: 34ft (10.3m). XR2 as above except **width**: 5ft 3.78in (1.62m); **track**: front 4ft 6.53in (1.38m), rear 4ft 4.72in (1.34m). **APPROXIMATE WEIGHTS**: 950 14cwt 3qtr 2lb (750kg), 1100 14cwt 3qtr 13lb (755kg), 1300 15cwt 1qtr 1lb (775kg), diesel 16cwt 1qtr 21lb (835kg). **CAPACITIES**: Fuel 7.5 gallons (34 litres), XR2 and all later models 8.8 gallons (40 litres).

Ford Fiesta mark 3

Launched in April 1989, this was a completely new car not a face-lifted model, and, although the overall length of the car was increased by only 4 inches, the wheelbase was 6 inches greater than the preceding Fiesta, enabling a new five-door variant to be introduced. The engine range continued to be a mix of Valencia and CVH engines, but the smaller engines were revised, with new capacities of 999cc and 1118cc, and new cylinder heads, designated HCS (High Compression Swirl). The swirling effect resulted in a better mix of fuel and air, and maximum power was produced at lower engine revolutions. All engines now featured electronic breakerless ignition, and 1.1 and 1.4 engines were available with catalytic converters. Eventually, of course, the sale of cars without catalytic converters would be banned.

The rear axle was of a new design,

Instrument layout.

featuring a torsion beam, and rear spring travel was reduced. The front strut suspension was retained, but with modifications to the lower wishbones. There were also revisions to the steering ratio and the option of power-assisted steering. ABS was offered as an option on most models.

The XR2i arrived in October 1989, with ventilated front disc brakes, front anti-roll bar, and one-piece moulded bumpers with auxiliary driving lights incorporated in the front bumper. Blue inserts in the bumpers and side mouldings completed its appearance. The RS Turbo, which arrived in June 1990, differed from the XR2 in that it had stiffer suspension, tighter steering, the Escort turbo engine but with smaller turbo unit, bonnet louvres, three spoke wheels and green instead of blue pinstriping. The RS Turbo was replaced in May 1992 by the RS 1800i, at which point the XR2i received the Zetec 16-valve engine.

Changes made in October 1992 included the move to white front indicator lens, and, for 1994, a driver's airbag was fitted to all models, with a passenger airbag available as an option. The bodyshell was reinforced with side impact beams, petrol-engined cars were

Five-door variant introduced with the mark 3 range.

fitted with engine immobiliser systems, and the XR2i was replaced by the Si available with 1.4 or 1.6 engines. Also in 1994, a Base model with 1.3 engine and many special editions were introduced. In 1995 more special editions were released, but the range was eventually reduced in preparation for the launch of the mark 4, which first appeared at the October 1995 Motor Show. The initial Mark 3 range comprised three-door 1.0 Popular, Popular Plus, 1.1 Popular Plus, L, LX, 1.8 diesel Popular Plus, L, five-door 1.0 Popular, 1.1 Popular Plus, LX, Ghia, 1.4 LX, Ghia, 1.8 diesel Popular Plus, LX. The 1.1 and 1.4 models were available with CTX automatic transmission. There followed major revisions to the range 1991.

Standard equipment for Popular Plus

and LX included radio (radio/cassette for LX), clock, variable intermittent wipe front wipers, fully reclining front seats with headrests, 60/40 split folding rear bench seat, inertia reel seatbelts, front door bins, glove box, three-speed heater blower, four face level vents adjustable for direction and airflow, front side window demisters, heated rear window, tailgate wash/wipe, reversing light, rear foglight, hazard warning flashers, and more. LX added wider side trim, bright insert in bumpers, sunroof, and, for petrol models, tachometer, mileage trip recorder. XR2i, in addition to LX, had front console, front seatback storage nets, height adjustable front seatbelt fixing points, electrically operated front door windows, remote tailgate release, central locking, narrow side trim with blue insert, wheelarch and sill extensions, tailgate spoiler, front fog and long-range driving lights.

PRICE WHEN INTRODUCED: 1.0 Popular three-door £5445, 1.1 LX three-door £7639, 1.4 LX five-door £8371, XR2i three-door £9995.

COLOURS (1990): Diamond White, Galaxy Blue, Wedgewood Blue, Radiant Red, Burgundy Red, and metallics Moondust Silver, Mercury Grey, Aztec Gold, Tasman Blue, Matisse Blue, Verona Green, Magenta.

XR2i with blue bumper and side trim inserts.

RS Turbo with green inserts.

ENGINE: Four-cylinder, 1.0 OHV, bore 68.7mm, stroke 67.5mm, 999cc (60.96in³), maximum bhp 44.3 at 5000rpm, single venturi carburettor. 1.1 OHV, bore 68.7mm, stroke 75.5mm, 1118cc (68.2in³), maximum bhp 53 at 5200rpm, twin venturi carburettor, 1.4 OHC, bore 77.2mm, stroke 74.3mm, 1392cc (84.9in³), maximum bhp 73 at 5600rpm, twin venturi carburettor. 1.6 OHC, bore 79.96mm, stroke 79.52mm, 1598cc (97.4in³), maximum bhp 88.5 at 5800rpm, twin venturi carburettor. XR2i as 1.6 except maximum bhp 108.6 at 6000rpm, multipoint fuel-injection. 1.8 diesel, bore 82.5mm, stroke 82mm, 1753cc (106.8in), maximum bhp 60 at 4800rpm. All above information relates to engines without catalytic converters.

GEARBOX: Five-speed, all-synchromesh, floor-mounted gear change. Ratios: 1.1 and 1.4 top 3.07. 4th 3.861, 3rd 5.359, 2nd 8.295, 1st 14.547, reverse 14.677; 1.6 top 2.89, 4th 3.633, 3rd 4.871, 2nd 7.308, 1st 12.048, reverse 13.809; 1.6i top 3.069, 4th 3.861, 3rd 5.177, 2nd 7.767, 1st 12.805, reverse 14.677; diesel top 2.728, 4th 3.411, 3rd 4.595, 2nd 6.857, 1st 11.309, reverse 12.996. 1.0, 1.1 and 1.4 with a four-speed gearbox, ratios as 1st to 4th of the five-speed gearbox (note 1.0 model only available with the four-speed gearbox). Front-wheel drive, final drive ratio all petrol models except 1.6 4.06:1, 1.6 (non-injection model) 3.82:1, diesel 3.59:1.

BRAKES: Dual-circuit, power-assisted with pressure limiting valve, front 9.5in discs, rear 7.5in drums, ABS optional.

STEERING: Rack and pinion.

TYRES: Popular and Popular Plus, 145SR x 13, LX 155/70 x 13, XR2i 185/60HR x 13. This is a general guide, 165 x 13 also available.

SUSPENSION: Front MacPherson struts, coil springs and telescopic shock absorbers, rear, trailing arms, coil springs, telescopic shock absorbers and torsion beam axle with Panhard rod.

DIMENSIONS: **Length**: 12ft 3.2in (3.74m); **width**: 5ft 3.4in (1.61m); **height**: 4ft 4.2in (1.325m); **wheelbase**: 8ft 0.3in (2.445m); **track**: front 4ft 6.7in (1.39m), rear 4ft 6.5in (1.385m); **ground clearance**: 5.51in (14cm); **turning circle**: 32ft 2.4in (9.8m). XR2 as above except **length**: 12ft 5.6in (3.8m), width 5ft 4.2in (1.63m); **track**: front 4ft 7.5in (1.41m), rear 4ft 6.3in (1.38m).

APPROXIMATE WEIGHTS: Popular three-door 1.0 15cwt 0qtr 18lb (770kg), LX five-door 16cwt 0qtr 16lb (820kg), Ghia five-door 1.4 16cwt 3qtr 9lb (855kg), XR2i 17cwt 2qtr 2lb (890kg).

CAPACITIES: Fuel 9.2 gallons (42 litres).

Escort mark 3 and Orion mark 1

Introduced in September 1980 with the slogan 'Simple is Efficient,' this was Ford's second ever front-wheel drive car, and was codenamed 'Erika.' Unlike most hatchbacks, the rear end of the car was shaped to create the impression that it had some form of boot. It did mean, however, that the tailgate did not extend down to bumper level, so there was a panel one had to lift luggage over, but this panel did increase the rigidity of the body. With three years having passed since the introduction of the Fiesta, much had been learned about the characteristics of front-wheel drive cars, and the transaxle, front suspension and some other components were derived from those used in that model, including the 1117cc engine. However, the Escort's 1300 and 1600 engines were of a new design, referred to as CVH (Compound Valve Hemispherical combustion chamber), and it would be three years before these engines started to appear in the Fiesta. There were refinements and the usual upgrades and model changes made during the Escort's lifetime. These included, in 1982: a five-speed gearbox was fitted to the 1600 engine, and available as an option on the 1300; automatic transmission was optional with the 1600 engine; L and Ghia received additional equipment; and there was the introduction of the short-lived 1100 economy and RS 1600i models. In 1983, all Escorts were fitted with a 10.5-gallon fuel tank, the XR3 became the XR3i, with fuel-injection instead of a carburettor, a cabriolet built by the German company Karmann was introduced as a 1300-, 1600 Ghia- or XR3i-based version, and a four-door saloon named the Orion was added to the range. Available as a GL or Ghia, and with the same equipment, doors and front bodywork as its Escort counterparts, the Orion had a different front grille, was nine inches longer than the Escort, had a different roof-line and rear seats, and greater rear passenger space.

Late in 1983 a diesel engine became

Escort 1.6 L.

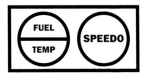

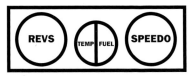

Instrument layout: Escort L model (top), and Ghia and XR3.

available for some models, then, in 1984, rear seats adopted a 60/40 split, new headrests were fitted, and power-assisted brakes became standard across the whole range. Also during 1984, the Popular car and estate models with the 1100 engine were introduced, along with a range of five-door estates. The RS Turbo replaced the RS 1600, the Orion range was expanded with the introduction of an L model, then, later in the year, special editions of the Escort started to appear, and more were produced in 1985 ahead of the launch of the revised Escort and Orion models in 1986. The 1980 range comprised: three-door, 1100 base, L, 1300 base, L, GL, Ghia, 1600 L, GL, Ghia, XR3, five-door 1100 base, L, 1300 base, L, GL Ghia, 1600 L, GL, Ghia. Estate 1100 base, L, 1300 base, L, GL, 1600 L, GL.

Standard equipment L included heater/demister with three-speed fan, radio, glove box, driver's lower parcel shelf, driver and passenger upper stowage shelves, front door stowage bins, reclining front seats with

1.6 Ghia.

headrests, two-speed wipers with intermittent wipe, driver's door mirror, reversing lights, rear fog lights, and heated rear window. GL added clock, centre console, mileage trip recorder, passenger door mirror, and bodyside moulding. Ghia, in addition to GL, had tachometer, variable intermittent wipe facility, seatback map pockets, remote control door mirrors, overriders, and sunroof. Optional extras included central locking, electrically operated front windows, tailgate wash/wipe (standard on XR3), overriders with headlight washers, and sunroof (standard on Ghia).

NUMBER PRODUCED: 1,857,000 Escort and Orion models.
PRICE WHEN INTRODUCED: 1100 L three-door £3695, 1300 GL five-door £4361, 1600 Ghia three-door £4883, XR3 £5123. Price in 1983: Escort 1300 GL five-door £5490, 1600 Ghia three-door £5803, Orion 1300 GL £5905, 1600 Ghia £7235.
COLOURS (1981): Diamond White, Midnight Blue, Nordic Blue, Dove Grey, Sunburst Red, Terracotta, Prairie Yellow, and metallics Strato Silver, Solar Gold, Cobalt Blue, Arctic Blue, Crystal Green, Forest Green, Aztec Bronze.
COLOURS (1984): Diamond White, Ocean Blue, Ceramic Blue, Sunburst Red, Cardinal Red, Coral Beige, Rio Brown, and metallics Strato Silver, Champagne Gold, Glacier Blue,

Caspian Blue, Jade Green, Nimbus Grey, Imperial Red.
ENGINE (1981): Four-cylinder, 1100 OHV, bore 73.96mm, stroke 64.98mm, 1117cc (68.16in^3), maximum bhp 54.4 at 5700rpm, Ford VV carburettor. 1300 OHC, bore 79.96mm, stroke 64.52mm, 1296cc (79.08in^3), maximum bhp 69 at 6000rpm, Ford VV carburettor. 1600 OHC, bore 79.96mm, stroke 79.52mm, 1597cc (97.45in^3), maximum bhp 79 at 5800rpm, Ford VV carburettor. XR3 as 1600 except, maximum bhp 96 at 6000rpm, Weber twin-choke carburettor.
GEARBOX (1981): Four-speed, all-synchromesh, floor-mounted gear change. Ratios: 1100 top 3.857, 3rd 5.481, 2nd 8.323, 1st 14.535, reverse 15.306; 1300 top 3.648, 3rd 5.184, 2nd 7.872, 1st 13.747, reverse 14.477; 1600 top 3.401, 3rd 4.547, 2nd 6.838, 1st 11.277, reverse 12.924; XR3 top 3.648, 3rd 4.877, 2nd 7.334, 1st 12.096, reverse 13.862. Front-wheel drive, final drive ratio 1100 4.06:1, 1300 3.840:1, 1600 3.580:1, XR3 3.84:1.
GEARBOX (1985): 1100 and 1300 as 1981. 1600, five-speed, all-synchromesh, top 2.72, 4th 3.401, 3rd 4.582, 2nd 6.838, 1st 11.277, reverse 12.960, final drive ratio 3.58:1
BRAKES: Dual-circuit with pressure limiting valve, front 9.45in discs, rear 7.1in drums,

RS Turbo.

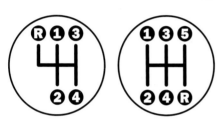

Gear change diagrams.

power-assisted on L models and above, ventilated front discs on 1600.

STEERING: Rack and pinion.

TYRES: 1100 145/80SR x 13, 1100 estate and all 1300 and 1600 models 155/80SR x 13, XR3 185/60HR x 14

SUSPENSION: Front MacPherson struts, lower wishbones, coil springs, telescopic shock absorbers, anti-roll bar (not 1100), rear independent with lower wishbones, trailing radius arms, coil springs, telescopic shock absorbers.

DIMENSIONS: **Length**: 13ft 0.3in (3.97m); **width**: 5ft 4.57in (1.64m); **height**: 4ft 7.12in (1.40m); **wheelbase**: 7ft 10.21in (2.39m); **track**: front 4ft 6.72in (1.39m), rear 4ft 8.3in (1.43m); **ground clearance**: 4.72in (12cm); **turning circle**: 34ft (10.5m). Estate as above except **length**: 13ft 2.78in (4.03m); **height**: 4ft 6.05in (1.37m). Orion as Escort except **length**: 13ft 9.08in (4.19m); **height**: 4ft 6.92in (1.39m).

CAPACITIES: Fuel 8.8 gallons (40 litres), 10.5 gallons (48 litres) from 1983.

Escort 1986 (revised mark 3 model)

Introduced in January 1986, and described by Ford as a 'face-lifted' mark 3 model, it

1.4 L, easily distinguished from earlier mark 3 models by its large polycarbonate bumpers.

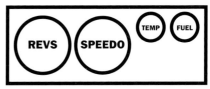

Instrument layout, GL, Ghia, XR3i.

has familiarly become known by the public as the mark 4, which was actually the designation given to the 1990 model by Ford. The bonnet now sloped further down at the front, reducing the size of the front grille, and, coupled with the new moulded one-piece polycarbonate bumpers, gave a much smoother look to the car. Both Escort and Orion models shared this style of new front end. At the back, as well as a moulded polycarbonate bumper replacing the original metal one, the ribbed rear lights became flattened, and the tailgate was reshaped to incorporate a lip, as first seen on the boot lid of the Orion in 1983. There were changes to the position of some front suspension components, the reintroduction of an OHV 1300 engine, and a new 1400 CVH to replace the previous 1300 CVH engine. Other changes included a revised instrument layout, improved security locking system, and the option of a braking system named SCS (Stop Control System). /this was a hydro-mechanical system rather than the electrical ABS (Anti-lock Braking System)

that was eventually adopted. Special editions started to appear in 1987, and 1400 and 1600 LX models were introduced and became a permanent part of the range. Then, in 1988, a 1.8 diesel engine replaced the previous 1.6, and all models received variable ratio steering. This was followed in 1989 by the introduction of CTX, more commonly called CVT (Continuously Variable Transmission) automatic transmission as an option for 1400 and 1600 engines, and there were general equipment upgrades all round.

The initial Escort range included three-door 1.1 Popular, 1.3 Popular, L, 1.4 L, GL, 1.6 XR3i, 1.6 diesel L, five-door 1.3 L, 1.4 L, GL, Ghia, 1.6 L, GL, Ghia, 1.6 diesel L, GL. Estate 1.1 Popular, 1.3 Popular, L, 1.4 L, GL, 1.6 L, GL, 1.6 diesel L, Cabriolet 1.6 Ghia, XR3i. The Orion range comprised 1.3 L, 1.4 L, GL, Ghia, 1.6 L, GL, Ghia, 1.6i Ghia, 1.6 diesel L, GL. Standard equipment for the L was generally as per the previous GL model, but now included clock, mileage trip recorder, passenger door mirror, and bodyside moulding. GL gained a centre console with cassette storage, tachometer, tinted glass, and an aerial incorporated into the rear windscreen. Ghia, in addition to GL, had a folding rear centre armrest, electrically operated front windows, central locking, and sunroof. All models except Popular now had a radio and cassette player instead of radio.

NUMBER PRODUCED: 1,885,000 (all Escort and Orion models 1980-89).
PRICE WHEN INTRODUCED: Escort 1300 L three-door £5930, 1400 GL five-door £6919, 1600 Ghia five-door £7746, Orion 1400 GL £7014, 1600 Ghia £8159.
COLOURS (1986): Diamond White, Maritime Blue, Galaxy Blue, Ivory, Rosso Red, Burgundy Red, Citrine Yellow, Black, and metallics Strato

Silver, Mercury Grey, Silica Gold, Chestnut, Regency Red, Willow Green, Crystal Blue, Azure Blue, Tropic Turquoise.

ENGINE (1986): Four-cylinder, 1100 OHV, bore 73.96mm, stroke 64.98mm, 1117cc (68.16in³), maximum bhp 49.6 at 5000rpm, Ford VV carburettor. 1300 OHV, bore 73.96mm, stroke 75.48mm, 1297cc (79.1in³), maximum bhp 59 at 5000rpm, Ford VV carburettor. 1400 OHC, bore 77.24mm, stroke 74.3mm, 1392cc (84.9in³), maximum bhp 73.8 at 5600rpm, Weber 2VDFTM carburettor. 1600 OHC, bore 79.96mm, stroke 79.52mm, 1597cc (97.45in³), maximum bhp 88.5 at 5800rpm, Weber 2VTLD carburettor. XR3i maximum bhp 103 at 6000rpm, Bosch K-Jetronic fuel-injection. 1600 diesel, bore 80mm, stroke 80mm, 1608cc (98.12in³), maximum bhp 52.97 at 4800rpm.

GEARBOX: Five-speed, all-synchromesh, floor-mounted gear change. Ratios: 1100 top 2.918, 4th 3.648, 3rd 5.069, 2nd 7.834, 1st 13.747, reverse 14.777; 1300 and 1400 top 2.918, 4th 3.648, 3rd 4.915, 2nd 7.334, 1st 12.096, reverse 13.901; 1400 with catalytic converter, top 2.903, 4th 3.652, 3rd 5.069, 2nd 7.845, 1st 13.759, reverse 13.882; 1600 top 2.72, 4th 3.401, 3rd 4.5827, 2nd 6.838, 1st 11.277, reverse 12.959; XR3i, top 3.245, 4th 4.057, 3rd 5.466, 2nd 8.156, 1st 13.451, reverse 15.457. Note 1100, 1300, 1400 with four-speed gearbox, ratios as 1st to 4th of five-speed gearbox. Front-wheel drive, final drive

Cabriolet.

ratio 1100, 1300, 1400 3.84:1, 1600 3.58:1, XR3i, 4.27:1, alternative ratio for 1100 4.06:1.

BRAKES: Dual-circuit, power-assisted, with optional controlled stop braking system, front 9.45in discs, rear 7.1in drums, ventilated front discs on 1400 and 1600.

STEERING: Rack and pinion.

TYRES: 1100 and 1300 145SR x 13, 1400 and 1600 models and all estates 155SR x 13, XR3i 185/60HR x 14

SUSPENSION: Front MacPherson struts, lower track control arms, coil springs, telescopic shock absorbers, anti-roll bar, rear independent with transverse arms, longitudinal tie-bars, coil springs, strut-type shock absorbers.

DIMENSIONS: Length: 13ft 3.5in (4.05m); **width:** 5ft 4.57in (1.64m); **height:** 4ft 5.9in (1.37m); **wheelbase:** 7ft 10.5in (2.40m); **track:** front 4ft 7.3in (1.405m), rear 4ft 8.1in (1.425m); **ground clearance:** 5.5in (14cm);

1.4 L.

The 2nd edition Orion featured the same frontal treatment as the Escort.

turning circle: 34ft 9.6in (10.6m). Estate as above except **length**: 13ft 4.6in (4.08m); **height**: 4ft 6.05in (1.37m). Orion as Escort except **length**: 13ft 9.5in (4.21m); **height**: 4ft 6.92in (1.39m).

APPROXIMATE WEIGHTS: Popular three-door 1100 16cwt 27lb (825kg), L five-door 1300 16cwt 3qtr 20lb (860kg), GL five-door 1400 17cwt 1qtr 19lb (885kg), Ghia five-door 1600 17cwt 2qtr 13lb (895kg), Orion GL 1400 17cwt 2qtr 25lb (900kg), Ghia 1600 17cwt 3qtr 7lb (905kg).

CAPACITIES: Fuel 10.5 gallons (48 litres). Boot Escort 12.7 ft^3 (0.36m^3) or 37.1ft^3 (1.05m^3), with rear seat folded down, estate 42.4ft^3 (1.2m^3). Orion 15.9ft^3 (0.45m^3).

Escort 1990 (mark 4)

Introduced in September 1990, and, as previously noted, given the designation mark 4 by Ford, this was an entirely

new model, with a larger body than its predecessor. It did, however, retain some of its predecessor's engines, with both the 1.4 and 1.6 being available with or without catalytic converters; the 1.1 engine was no longer available. As well as a new body there was new rear suspension, with both front and rear now based on that used in the Fiesta. An L model was introduced in 1991 to fit in between the Popular and LX models, with the LX gaining a tachometer, electric front windows and more. Shortly after this an S model appeared, an XR3i had not been included in the initial range. Special editions started to appear later in the year, and there were equipment upgrades, with LX models now having a height adjustable driver's seat, rear spoiler and two-tone paintwork, with the lower half of the body painted mid-grey. In November 1991 the RS2000 was launched. It had a 16-valve, twin OHC engine with fuel-injection and a catalytic converter. It also featured ABS, power-assisted steering, Recaro sports seats, alloy wheels, etc.

February 1992 saw the introduction of an entirely new engine. Initially available as a 1.8 16v, it would go on to be available as a 1.6 16v following the introduction of a new Escort in late 1992. In the meantime, this new engine, called Zetec, was fitted into the reintroduced XR3i and the LX and Ghia models. In June 1992, the RS Cosworth 4

RS with large bi-plane rear spoiler.

Cabriolet

Instrument layout GLX, Ghia.

x 4 with a turbo-charged twin-cam 1993cc engine was launched. It was immediately distinguished from the XR3i by its unique whale-tail spoiler, similar to that fitted to the Sierra RS Cosworth. Both XR3i and Cosworth had different frontal treatment to other Escorts, including the fitting of front indicators into the bumper instead of next to the headlights.

The initial range comprised: Escort three-door 1.3 Popular, LX, 1.8 diesel Popular, five-door 1.3 Popular, LX, GLX, Ghia, 1.4 and 1.6 LX, GLX, Ghia, 1.8 diesel Popular, LX, GLX, Ghia. Estate 1.3 Popular, LX, GLX, 1.4 LX, GLX, 1.6 LX, GLX, Ghia, 1.8 diesel Popular, LX, GLX. Cabriolet 1.6. The Orion range consisted of 1.3, 1.4, 1.6 petrol and 1.8 diesel LX, GLX, Ghia saloons. Standard equipment for Popular included radio, clock, mileage trip recorder, two-speed wipers with intermittent wipe, tailgate wash/wipe, reclining front seats

with headrests, height adjustable inertia reel front seatbelts, centre console, front door bins, driver's side lower parcel tray, passenger glove box and upper stowage tray, removable rear parcel tray, remotely controlled door mirrors, grey bumpers and bodyside moulding. LX added cigarette lighter, glove box with lid, vanity mirror on passenger sun visor, central door locking, remote tailgate release, 60/40 split rear seatback, tinted glass, sunroof. GLX, in addition to LX, had tachometer, variable intermittent wipers, courtesy lights with delayed switch-off operated by all doors, electrically operated and heated door mirrors. Ghia added front footwell courtesy lights, adjustable lumbar support for front seats, height adjustable driver's seat, body-coloured bumpers, and more.

PRICE WHEN INTRODUCED: Escort Popular 1.3 three door £7580, LX 1.3 five-door £9040, Ghia 1.3 five-door £10,740, Ghia 1.6 estate £12,460, Orion LX 1.3 £9310, Ghia 1.6 £12,310.

XR3i model, with indicators in the front bumper.

COLOURS (1990): Diamond White, Galaxy Blue, Wedgewood Blue, Burgundy Red, Radiant Red, Black, and metallics Moondust Silver, Mercury Grey, Aztec Gold, Tasman Blue, Matisse Blue, Verona Green, Firnwood, Magenta.

ENGINE (1990): Four-cylinder, 1.3 OHV, bore 73.96mm, stroke 75.48mm, 1297cc (79.1in^3), maximum 64PS at 5000rpm, Ford VV carburettor. 1.4 OHC, bore 77.24mm, stroke 74.3mm, 1392cc (84.9in^3), maximum 73PS at 5500rpm, twin-choke carburettor, with catalytic converter 71PS at 5600rpm, Ford electronic single-point fuel-injection. 1.6 OHC, bore 79.96mm, stroke 79.52mm, 1597cc (97.45in^3), maximum 90PS at 5800rpm, Weber twin-choke carburettor. 1600i bore 80mm, stroke 79.5mm, 1596cc (97.39in^3), maximum 108PS at 6000rpm, electronic fuel-injection with EEC IV engine management system, with catalytic converter 105PS at 6000rpm. 1800 diesel, bore 82.5mm, stroke 82mm, 1753cc (106.97in^3), maximum 60PS at 4800rpm.

GEARBOX: Five-speed, all-synchromesh, floor-mounted gear change. Ratios: 1.3 top 3.086, 4th 3.857, 3rd 5.197, 2nd 7.755, 1st 12.789, reverse 14.697; 1.4 top 3.086, 4th 3.857, 3rd 5.359, 2nd 8.282, 1st 14.535, reverse 14.697; 1.6 top 2.906, 4th 3.633, 3rd 4.895,

Gear change diagram.

2nd 7.304, 1st 12.046, reverse 13.843; diesel top 2.728, 4th 3.411, 3rd 4.595, 2nd 6.857, 1st 12.852, reverse 12.996. Front-wheel drive, final drive ratio 1.3 and 1.4 with catalytic converter, 4.06:1, 1.6 3.82:1, diesel 3.59:1.

BRAKES: Dual-circuit, power-assisted, with optional anti-lock braking system, front 9.45in discs, rear 7.1in drums, ventilated front discs on 1400 and 1600.

STEERING: Rack and pinion.

TYRES: Popular 155SR x 13, cabriolet 185/60 HR x 14, all other models 175/70 x 13.

SUSPENSION: Front MacPherson struts, coil

springs with forward mounted stabiliser bar, anti-roll bar on 1.6 models, rear independent with swinging arms, longitudinal tie-bars, coil springs, strut-type shock absorbers. **DIMENSIONS: Length**: 13ft 2.9in (4.035m); **width**: 5ft 6.5in (1.69m); **height**: 4ft 6.9in (1.395m); **wheelbase**: 8ft 3.4in (2.525m); **track**: front 4ft 8.7in (1.44m), rear 4ft 9.5in (1.46m); **turning circle**: 32ft 10in (10m). Estate as above except **length**: 14ft 0.1in (4.27m); **height**: 4ft 7.7in (1.451m). Orion as Escort except **length**: 13ft 10.5in (4.229m).
APPROXIMATE WEIGHTS: Escort Popular three-door 1.3, 17cwt 3qtr 8lb (905kg), LX three-door 1.4 (catalyst), 18cwt 3qtr 6lb (955kg), GLX five-door 1.6, 19cwt 2qtr 10lb (995kg), estate 1.4 LX (catalyst), 1ton 0cwt 1qtr 3lb (1030kg), Orion 1.4 LX (catalyst), 19cwt 3qtr 15lb (1010kg), GLX 1.6 (catalyst), 1ton 0cwt 20lb (1025kg).
CAPACITIES: Fuel 12.1 gallons (55 litres). Boot Escort 13.4ft^3 (0.38m^3), estate 16.3ft^3 (0.46m^3). Orion 17.3ft^3 (0.49m^3).

Escort 1992

Introduced in September 1992, this was an updated version of the 1990 model. There is some confusion as to whether this should be designated as a mark 4 (revised) or a mark 5 model. It featured a reinforced bodyshell, using thicker steel in the front bulkhead, side impact beams in front and rear doors, and other structural changes to keep its occupants safer. It also had a restyled front, with the bonnet now incorporating the front grille opening, and white front indicators and larger rear lights for the Escort. The Orion and estate retained their original rear lights, and the XR3i, although adopting the new bonnet, continued with the amber front indicators incorporated into the front bumper. Mechanical changes included the introduction of the 1.6 Zeta engine, and modifications to the 1.3 to enable it to run with a catalytic converter. A front anti-roll bar was now standard on all but 1.3 models. The 1.6 and 1.8 models now had a rear anti-roll bar and power-assisted steering, and all models had revised door locking systems to improve vehicle security, with shielded door locks, anti-theft alarms and, on most models, engine immobilisers.

In 1993 a host of new models appeared, including a 1.8 Si cabriolet and two 1.6 special editions: Silhouette and Mistral. Also during 1993 turbo diesel LX and Ghia models were introduced, plus 1.8 Ghia Si and RS2000 4x4. Towards the end of the year the Orion name

The 1992 Escort cabriolet had the oval grille that would remain a feature of all Escorts until they were discontinued.

was dropped, with those models now being called Escort saloon.

More special editions appeared in 1994, including Azura, Mistral, Sapphire and Equipe. This was often seen as an indication that Ford was about to launch a revised model, which it did in 1995.

The initial 1992 Escort range comprised: three-door 1.3 base, 1.4 base, L, LX, 1.8 LX, XR3i, RS2000, five-door 1.3 base, 1.4 base, L, LX, Ghia, 1.6 L, LX, Ghia, 1.8 LX, Ghia, 1.8 diesel base, L, LX. Estate, 1.3 base, 1.4 base, L, LX, 1.6 L, LX Ghia, 1.8 LX, Ghia, 1.8 diesel base, L, LX. The Orion range comprised 1.4, 1.6, 1.8 LX, Ghia 1.8 diesel LX. Standard equipment was generally as per the previous models and incorporated the 1991 changes, including the equipment and styling upgrades to the LX model and the inclusion of rear headrests and alloy wheels for Ghia models.

PRICE WHEN INTRODUCED: Escort 1.3 three-door £8389, 1.4 five-door £8988, 1.4 LX five-door £10,550, 1.6 Ghia five-door £11,904, Orion 1.6 LX £11,261, 1.8 Ghia £12,144.

COLOURS (1993): Balliol Blue, Diamond White, Radiant Red, Aporto Red, Black, and metallics Moondust Silver, Aqua Foam, Nouveau Red, Levante Grey, Tourmaline Green, Pacifica Blue (XR3i only). Cabriolet colours were Diamond White, Zinc Yellow, and metallics Moondust Silver, Imperial Blue, Coral Red, Spring Green, Ash Black.

Gear change diagram.

ENGINE: Four-cylinder with catalytic converters for petrol engines, 1.3, 1.4 and 1.8 diesel as 1990 models. 1.6 DOHC, bore 76mm, stroke 88mm, 1597cc ($97.45in^3$), maximum 90PS at 5500rpm, electronic fuel-injection with EEC IV engine management system. 1.8 DOHC, bore 80.6mm, stroke 88mm, 1796cc ($109.6in^3$), maximum 105PS at 5500rpm, electronic fuel-injection with EEC IV engine management system.

GEARBOX: All-synchromesh, 1.3, 1.4 and 1.6 as 1990 models, 1.8 as 1.6 models. Front-wheel drive, final drive ratio 1.3 and 1.4 4.06:1, 1.6 and 1.8 3.82:1, diesel 3.59:1.

BRAKES: Dual-circuit, power-assisted, with optional anti-lock braking system, front 9.5in discs, rear 7in drums.

Top XR3i, bottom Orion LX.

STEERING: Rack and pinion, power-assisted on 1.6, 1.8 and 1.4 Ghia.

TYRES: Escort 155SR x 13, L 175/70 x 13, all other models 185/60 HR x 14.

SUSPENSION: Front MacPherson struts, coil springs with forward-mounted stabiliser bar,

Above: Orion LX. Below, this black Escort is a Chicane model.

anti-roll bar on 1.6, 1.8 and diesel models, rear MacPherson strut with coil springs, anti-roll bar on 1.6 and 1.8.
DIMENSIONS: As 1990 models.
CAPACITIES: As 1990 models.

Escort 1995 (mark 5)

Introduced in January 1995, and replaced by the Ford Focus in 1998, two new models of the Escort, the Flight and Finesse, with a choice of 1.6 petrol or 1.8 diesel and available as a hatchback or estate, were the only models available after January 1999. Although discontinued in July 2000, some cars were still being sold from dealer stock later than this. Sometimes referred to as the second update or third version of 1990 model, the 1995 Escort featured a revised front grille, body-coloured bumpers (except Encore), oval side repeater indicators, revised door handles and mirrors, and mechanical changes to the rear axle, front castor angle, and other suspension changes. Inside was a revised dashboard with wood effect finish on the Ghia model. The whole range was revised, with the basic model now called Encore, and the XR3i was deleted. The RS2000 arrived in April 1995, special editions soon started to appear, and the L was renamed CL in 1997.

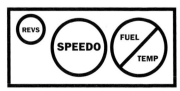

Instrument layout. Note that some models did not have a revolution counter.

The 1995 range comprised: three-door 1.3 Encore, 1.4 Encore, L, LX, 1.6 L, LX, Si, 1.8 Si, 1.8 diesel Encore, L, LX; five-door 1.3 Encore, 1.4 Encore, L, LX, 1.6 L, LX, Si, Ghia, 1.8 LX, Si, Ghia, 1.8 diesel Encore, L, LX, Ghia; four-door, 1.4 L, LX, 1.6 L, LX, Ghia, 1.8 Ghia, 1.8 diesel L, LX, Ghia; estate 1.3 Encore, 1.4 Encore, L, LX, 1.6 L, LX, Si, Ghia, 1.8 LX, Si, Ghia, 1.8 diesel, Encore, L, LX, Ghia. Standard equipment for Encore included, radio/cassette

RS2000 4x4.

player, two-speed wipers with intermittent wipe, tailgate wash/wipe, fully reclining front seats with headrests, split folding rear seat, passenger upper and driver lower fascia stowage trays, glove box, door bins, centre console, remotely controlled door mirrors, front-door-operated courtesy lights, heated rear window. LX added tachometer, central locking,

Escort Chicane special edition. The small reflectors below the rear lights were fitted by the author.

electrically operated front windows. Ghia, in addition to LX, had variable intermittent wipe front wipers, body-coloured electrically heated and operated door mirrors, courtesy lights with delayed switch-off operated by all doors, wood-style instrument and gearlever surround. Si has sports instrument cluster with white dials and red pointers, and, in addition to Ghia, front fog lights, special steering wheel, and more. Optional extras for some models included quick-clear heated windscreen, heated washer jets, air-conditioning, front passenger airbag, and ABS.

Top is a Ghia, bottom is a GTi, identified by its front fog lights.

PRICE WHEN INTRODUCED: Encore 1.3 three-door £9495, LX 1.4 five-door £11,740, Ghia 1.6 four-door £12,865.

COLOURS (1995): Ontario Blue, Diamond White, Radiant Red, Dark Maroon, and metallics Moondust Silver, Nouveau Red, Petrol Blue, State Blue, Auralis Blue, Tourmaline Green, Alberto Green, Dark Aubergine, Ash Black. Not all colours available on all models.

ENGINE: Four-cylinder with fuel-injection, catalytic converters for petrol engines. 1.3 OHV, bore 73.96mm, stroke 75.48mm, 1297cc (79.1in³), maximum 60PS at 5000rpm. 1.4 OHC, bore 77.24mm, stroke 74.3mm, 1392cc (84.9in³), maximum 75PS at 5500rpm. 1.6 DOHC, bore 76mm, stroke 88mm, 1597cc (97.45in³), maximum 90PS at 5500rpm. 1.8 DOHC, bore 80.6mm, stroke 88mm, 1796cc (109.6in³), maximum 105PS at 5500rpm. 1800 diesel, bore 82.5mm, stroke 82mm, 1753cc (106.97in³), maximum 60PS at 4800rpm.

GEARBOX: Five-speed, all-synchromesh, floor-mounted gear change. Ratios: 1.3 top 3.086, 4th 3.857, 3rd 5.197, 2nd 7.755, 1st 12.789, reverse 14.697; 1.4 top 3.086, 4th 3.857, 3rd 5.359, 2nd 8.282, 1st 14.535, reverse 14.697; 1.6 and 1.8 top 2.906, 4th 3.633, 3rd 4.895, 2nd 7.304, 1st 12.046, reverse 13.843; diesel top 2.728, 4th 3.411, 3rd 4.595, 2nd 6.857, 1st 12.852, reverse 12.996. Front-wheel drive, final drive ratio 1.3 and 1.4 4.06:1, 1.6 and 1.8 3.82:1, diesel 3.59:1.

BRAKES: Dual-circuit, power-assisted, front 9.5in discs, rear 7in drums, anti-lock braking system optional.

STEERING: Rack and pinion, power-assisted on all but Encore and L 1.3 and 1.4 models.

TYRES: Encore 155/70SR x 13, L and Encore diesel and estate 175/70 x 13, LX 175/65HR x 14, Ghia and Si 185/60HR x 14.

SUSPENSION: Front, MacPherson struts, coil springs with forward-mounted stabiliser bar, anti-roll bar, rear MacPherson strut with coil springs and twist beam member rear axle.

DIMENSIONS: **Length**: 13ft 6.9in (4.138m); **width**: 5ft 6.5in (1.69m); **height**: 4ft 6.9in (1.395m); **wheelbase**: 8ft 3.4in (2.525m); **track**: front 4ft 8.7in (1.44m), rear 4ft 9.5in (1.46m); **ground clearance**: 4.7in (12cm); **turning circle**: 32ft 10in (10m). Estate as above except **length**: 14ft 1.37in (4.302m); **height**: 4ft 9.5in (1.46m). Saloon as hatchback except **length**: 14ft 1.09in (4.295m).

CAPACITIES: Fuel 12.1 gallons (55 litres). Boot hatchback 13.4ft³ (0.38m³), estate 16.3ft³ (0.46m³) or hatchback 40ft³ (1.13m³), estate 50.3ft³ (1.425m³) with rear seat folded down and loaded to roof height, saloon 17.3ft³ (0.49m³).

Ford Sierra

Introduced in October 1982 to replace the Ford Cortina, the Sierra name was already in use by the Dutton Car Company, which was producing an estate car bodykit using Escort mark 1/2 running gear. A subsequent court decision allowed Dutton to continue using the name provided it included the word 'kit.' The styling of the Ford Sierra, which quickly earned the nickname 'jellymould,' was subject to mixed reactions. The decision to continue with rear-wheel drive when its main rival, the Vauxhall Cavalier, had changed to front-wheel drive, together with the fact that the Cavalier was available as a four-door saloon or five-door hatchback whereas the Sierra was available only as a hatchback or estate, didn't help either. Mechanically, the engines were carried over from the Cortina, but the front suspension reverted to MacPherson strut and the rear suspension was a development of that used on the Granada. Other improvements over the Cortina included more interior space, and five-speed gearboxes for some models, there were also economy engines introduced, a 1.6 petrol with electronic ignition and the 2.3 diesel used in the Granada.

Early complaints about susceptibility to crosswinds resulted in the introduction of plastic 'ears' to the rear quarter windows of five-door Sierras. Other changes made included the introduction of three-door basic Sierra, L and the XR4i models in 1983, new economy engines in 1984, followed by the restyling of the front end with the adoption of the Ghia-type smooth radiator panel replacing the three-bar slotted grille on all but the basic and diesel models. There were also equipment upgrades at this time, with GL models being fitted with a tachometer and five-speed gearbox. The XR4i received central

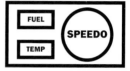

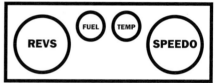

Instrument layout (1982) L, GL models (top), and (1990) LX, GLX, GLS, Ghia models.

Early Sierra with slatted front grille.

locking, electric windows, sunroof. 1985 saw the introduction of a 2000i S based on the GL, the five-door XR4x4 with permanent four-wheel drive replaced the three-door XR4i, and there were further equipment upgrades to some models. A major change occurred in 1987. There were revisions to the design, including a lower bonnet line extending down to bumper level, flush-fitting headlights, larger glass area and the introduction of the Sierra Sapphire four-door saloons. Other changes included discontinuing the 1.3 engine, stiffer suspension, revised instruments and switchgear, improved security locking system, and the availability of ABS.

In 1988 the L models received a sunroof and tinted glass, LX had central locking, larger wheels, and electric front windows, and GLS had headlight wash/wipe. The range was revised in 1990, and there were changes to engine specifications in 1991. The Sierra was discontinued in 1993 and replaced by the front-wheel drive Mondeo.

The initial range comprised 1.3 Sierra and L hatchbacks and the following hatchbacks and estates: 1.6 Sierra, L, GL, Ghia, 2.0 GL, Ghia, 2.3 GL, Ghia, 2.3 diesel Sierra, L, and GL. The 1990 range comprised Sapphire 1.6 Classic, LX , 1.8 and 2.0 LX, GLX, 2.0 EFi GLX, GLS, Ghia, 2000E, Ghia 4x4, 1.8 diesel Classic, LX, GLX, Sierra hatchbacks and estates, 1.6 Laser,

LX, 1.8 and 2.0 LX, GLX, 2.0 EFi, GLX, Ghia, 1.8 diesel Laser, LX, GLX and the following hatchbacks only: 2.0 EFi GLS, XR, and XR4x4. Standard equipment included reclining front seats, front door bins, glove box, driver's door mirror, heated rear window, rear fog lights, reversing lights, side repeater indicators, and hazard warning flashers. L added clock, radio, intermittent wipe front wipers, front seat headrests, passenger door mirror, bodyside moulding. GL, in addition to L, had driver's seat lumbar adjustment, lockable glove box, coin box in fascia, centre rear armrest, halogen headlights, body-coloured bumpers. Ghia, in addition to GL, had tachometer, radio/cassette player, variable intermittent wipers, passenger seat lumbar adjustment, driver's seat height adjustment, rear seat headrests, seatback map pockets, carpeted lower door,

Top: five-door XR 4x4 which replaced the three-door. Above: XR4i.

144

electrically adjustable driver and passenger door mirrors, wide bodyside moulding, sunroof, front bumpers with fog lights, and overriders. Optional extras were automatic transmission for 1.6, 2.0 and 2.3 petrol engines, power-assisted steering for all cars with 2.0 and 2.3 engines, central locking, heated driver's seat, seat height adjustment, headlight washers, sunroof, tailgate wash/wipe. For 1990 most models had a tachometer, centre console, radio/cassette player, delayed courtesy light switch-off, anti-theft alarm, integral front fog lights, front and rear wheelarch liners, headlight wash/wipe, and rear screen wash/wipe.

PRICES (1982): Sierra hatchback, 1.3 L £5234, 1.6 L £5522, 2.0 Ghia £7709, estates 1.6 L £5548, 2.3 Ghia £9034.
PRICES (1990): Sierra hatchback, 1.6 Laser £9380, 1.6LX £9995, Ghia 2.0 EFi £14,620, estate 1.8 GLX £12,175, Sapphire 1.6LX £9995, 2.0EFi £14,620.
COLOURS (1982): Diamond White, Coral Beige, Rio Brown, Pine Green, Cardinal Red, Polar Grey, Baltic Blue*, Black, and metallics Strato Silver, Graphite Grey, Champagne Gold, Solar Gold*, Crystal Green, Forest Green*, Imperial Red, Glacier Blue, Caspian Blue (* not 2.3 V6 or 2.3 diesel).
COLOURS (1987): Diamond White, Ivory, Citrine Yellow, Maritime Blue, Galaxy Blue,

The top two cars are Sierra RS models, bottom is a Sapphire Cosworth.

Rosso Red, Burgundy Red, Black, and metallics Strato Silver, Silica Gold, Willow Green, Crystal Blue, Regency Red, Chestnut, Mercury Grey. Not all colours available for some models.

ENGINE (1984): Four-cylinder, OHC, 1.3, bore 79mm, stroke 66mm, 1294cc (78.9in^3), maximum bhp 60 at 5700rpm, Ford VV carburettor. 1.6, bore 87.65mm, stroke 66mm, 1593cc (97.2in^3), maximum bhp 74 at 5300rpm, Ford VV carburettor. 2.0, bore 90.82mm, stroke 76.95mm, 1993cc (121.6in^3), maximum bhp 103 at 5200rpm, Weber carburettor. 2.3 diesel, OHV, bore 94mm, stroke 83mm, 2304cc (140.6in^3), maximum bhp 65.7 at 4200rpm, Bosch injection. Six-cylinder 2.3 (V6 OHC), bore 90mm, stroke 60.14mm, 2294cc (139.98in^3), maximum bhp 112 at 5300rpm, Solex twin-choke 35/35 carburettor. 2.8 (V6 OHV), bore 93mm, stroke 68.5mm, 2792cc (170.4in^3), maximum 150 at 5700rpm, Bosch fuel-injection.

GEARBOX: Four-speed, all-synchromesh, floor-mounted gear change. Ratios: 1.3 top 3.77, 3rd 5.353, 2nd 8.219, 1st 13.798, reverse 15.947; 1.6 top 3.62, 3rd 5.068, 2nd 7.276, 1st 12.96, reverse 12.018; 2.0 top 3.38, 3rd 4.631, 2nd 6.659, 1st 12.337, reverse 12.371. Five-speed, all-synchromesh. 2.3 diesel, top 2.575, 4th 3.14, 3rd 4.082, 2nd 7.285, 1st 12.277, reverse 11.492; 2.8 top 2.99, 4th 3.62, 4th 4.55, 2nd 6.55, 1st 12.16, reverse 12.20.

REAR AXLE: Hypoid bevel, semi-floating. Ratios: 1.3 3.77:1, 1.6 3.62:1, 2.0 3.38:1,

The changing faces of the Sierra.

2.8 3.62:1, 2.3 petrol, hatchback, 3.14:1, estate 3.38:1, 2.3 diesel 3.14:1.

ENGINE (1990): Four-cylinder with fuel-injection systems, 1.6i CVH, bore 80mm, stroke 79.5mm, 1598cc (97.5in^3), maximum 80PS at 5500rpm; 1.8i, bore 86.2mm, stroke 76.95mm, 1796cc (109.6in^3), maximum 90PS at 5250rpm; 2.0i, bore 90.8mm, stroke 77mm, 1993cc (121.6in^3), maximum 100PS at 5100rpm; Cosworth 220 PS at 6000rpm, 2.0i 16v, bore 86mm, stroke 86mm, 1998cc (121.9in^3), maximum 120PS at 5500rpm; 1.8 diesel, bore 82.5mm, stroke 82mm, 1753cc (106.97in^3), maximum 75PS at 4500rpm.

GEARBOX: Five-speed, all-synchromesh. Ratios: 1.6 top 3.214, 4th 3.92, 3rd 5.37,

2nd 7.724, 1st 14.308, reverse 14.347; 1.8 top 2.954, 4th 3.62, 3rd 5.017, 2nd 7.124, 1st 13.213, reverse 13.249; 2.0 top 2.968, 4th 3.62, 3rd 4.959, 2nd 7.131, 1st 13.213, reverse 13.249; 2.0 16v, top 2.968, 4th 3.62, 3rd 4.851, 2nd 7.53, 1st 14.082, reverse 12.706; 1.8 diesel, top 2.772, 4th 3.38, 3rd 4.631, 2nd 6.659, 1st 12.337, reverse 12.371 (with 3.62:1 axle as 2.0 engine).

REAR AXLE: 1.6, 3.92:1, 2.0, 3.62:1, 2.0 16v, 3.62:1 or 3.92:1, 1.8 diesel, 3.38:1 or 3.62:1.

BRAKES: Dual-circuit, power-assisted, front 9.45in discs, 1300 and 1600 rear 8in drums, 2000 and 2300 rear 9in drums.

STEERING: Rack and pinion, safety steering column, anti-theft lock, power-assistance optional.

TYRES: 165 x 13 hatchbacks, 175 x 13 estates.

SUSPENSION: Front, MacPherson struts with coil springs, rearward mounted anti-roll bar, rear independent semi-trailing arm/coil springs and twin-tube shock absorbers.

DIMENSIONS: Saloon **length:** 14ft 7.9in (4.467m); **width:** 5ft 6.9in (1.7m) or 6ft 3.6in (1.92m) with mirrors; **height:** 4ft 5.5in (1.359m); **wheelbase:** 8ft 6.7in (2.608m); **track:** front 4ft 9in (1.45m), rear 4ft 9.9in (1.47m); **ground clearance:** 4.7in (12cm); **turning circle:** 34ft 8in (10.6m). Hatchback as saloon except **length:** 14ft 6.2in (4.425m).

Gear change diagrams.

Estate as saloon except **length:** 14ft 9.6in (4.511m); **height:** 4ft 6.6in (1.386m).

APPROXIMATE WEIGHTS: Saloon 2.0 Ghia 1ton 2cwt 1qtr 10lb (1135kg), hatchback 1.6L 1ton 1qtr 25lb (1040kg), 2.0GLS 1ton 1cwt 2qtr 6lb(1095kg), estate 1.6L 1ton 1cwt 2qtr 18lb (1100kg), 2.0 Ghia 1ton 3cwt 1qtr 9lb (1185kg).

CAPACITIES: Fuel 13.2 gallons (60 litres). Boot, saloon 14.6ft³ (0.41m³), hatchback 13.6ft³ (0.385m³), estate 15.1ft³ (0.428m³) or hatchback 42.2ft³ (1.195m³), estate 51.8ft³ (1.467m³) with rear seat folded down.

The car on this page is a 1.6L estate.

Sierra Sapphire.

1.6 L Estate.

Ford Probe

Introduced in March 1994, seven years after the Capri had been discontinued, this was Ford's venture back into the coupé market for the UK. It was discontinued in 1998 and replaced by the Ford Cougar. The Probe was built in the USA, where it had already been available for two years, and was based around the Mazda MX6 coupé, which itself had been derived from the Mazda 626, but the Probe used different suspension similar to that used in the Mondeo. There were just two versions available with equipment levels set according to engine size. Standard equipment for the 2.0 included oil pressure gauge, voltmeter, tachometer, radio/cassette player, centre console with clock, rake adjustable steering column, fully reclining front seats with headrests, driver and front passenger airbags, split folding rear seatback, electrically operated and heated door mirrors, heated rear window, tailgate wash/wipe, remotely operated fuel filler flap and tailgate release, central locking, alarm and engine immobiliser, side impact bars. The 2.5 model added upgraded radio/cassette player, leather-covered steering wheel and gear knob, cruise control, sunroof, body-coloured side cladding, and more.

PRICE WHEN INTRODUCED: 2.0 £15,995, 2.5 £19,350.

COLOURS (1994): Vibrant White, Rio Red, Ebony Black, and metallics Electric Blue, Electric Currant Red, Light Aspen Silver, Teal Mist.

ENGINE: 2.0, four-cylinder, DOHC, bore 83mm, stroke 92mm, 1991cc (121.5in^3), maximum bhp 118 at 5500rpm, Mitsubishi electronic fuel-injection. 2.5 V6, DOHC, bore 84.5mm, stroke 74.2mm, 2497cc (152.4in^3) maximum bhp 163.6 at 5600rpm, Nissan electronic fuel-injection.

GEARBOX: Five-speed, all-synchromesh, floor-mounted gear change. Ratios: 2.0, top 3.161, 4th 3.995 3rd 5.399, 2nd 8.034, 1st 14.531, reverse 13.916; 2.5, top 3.424, 4th 4.522, 3rd 5.751, 2nd 8.034, 1st 14.531, reverse 13.916. Front-wheel drive, final drive ratio both models 4.39:1.

BRAKES: Power-assisted with anti-lock system, front 10.16in ventilated discs, rear 10.16in discs.

STEERING: Rack and pinion, power-assisted speed sensitive.

TYRES: 2.0 205/55 x 15, 2.5 225/50 x 16.

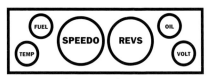

Instrument layout.

Note both models supplied with 'spacesaver' spare wheels.

SUSPENSION: Front MacPherson struts with triangulated lower track control arms and anti-roll bar, rear Quadralink independent with anti-roll bar.

DIMENSIONS: **Length**: 14ft 10.8in (4.54m); **width**: 5ft 9.9in (1.78m); **height**: 4ft 3.57in (1.131m); **wheelbase**: 8ft 6.8in (2.61m); **track**: front and rear 4ft 11.8in (1.52m); **ground clearance**: 6.3in (16cm); **turning circle**: 36.8ft (11.2m).

APPROXIMATE WEIGHTS: 2.0 1ton 3cwt 3qtr 19lb (1215kg), 2.5 1ton 5cwt 0qtr 22lb (1280kg).

CAPACITIES: Fuel 13 gallons (59 litres). Boot 10.8in^3 (0.396m^3) or 36.4in^3 (1.0m^3) with rear seatback folded down.

Ford Mondeo

Introduced in March 1993 as a four-door saloon and five-door hatchback, with an estate following in June 1993, the Mondeo replaced the Sierra and saw the switch to front-wheel drive. Ford's competitors had already introduced this with the 1981 Vauxhall Cavalier, the 1984 Austin Montego, the 1987 Peugeot 405, and the 1990 Nissan Primera. Mechanically, the Mondeo featured a new range of engines designed to fit transversally, allowing overall length to be marginally reduced. Also new was the rear suspension, as there was no requirement for a conventional rear axle and propshaft as used in the Sierra. January 1994 saw the arrival of the V6 Duratec engine, and soon afterwards the start of the special editions, the Aspen similar to the base model, Mistral similar to the 1.6LX, and Ultima based on the Ghia. The Ultima name was also used for a Scorpio model. A further Mondeo model, the Verona, available from 1995, was available with the 1.8 16v petrol or 1.8 turbo diesel engines, there was a choice of two colours: Juice Green and Mistral Blue.

The Mondeo underwent a restyle in 1996

This page and overleaf: Mondeo saloon; hatchback.

at which time there were changes to the interior, new engines and improvements to safety features. The 1993 range comprised saloon and hatchback 1.6 and 1.8 diesel Mondeo, LX and GLX, 1.8 LX, GLX, 2.0 GLX, Si and Ghia, and the following estates: 1.6, 1.8 and 1.8 diesel LX and GLX, 2.0 GLX and Ghia. Standard equipment for all models included radio/cassette player, reclining front seats with side stowage bins and adjustable headrests, door bins, illuminated lockable glove box, 60/40 split rear seatback, driver and passenger door mirrors (electrically heated and operated on GLX, Si Ghia), heated rear window, tinted glass, power-assisted steering with rake and reach adjustable steering column, steering wheel airbag, central locking with torch key, alarm system, rear fog lights, reversing lights, side repeater indicators, hazard warning flashers, and, for all models LX and above, tachometer, seatback map pockets, sunroof, electrically operated front door windows. GLX, S, and Ghia add variable intermittent wipe front windscreen wipers, driver's seat electric height adjustment, front seat adjustable lumbar support, passenger under seat stowage tray, rear seat headrests and folding centre armrest. Optional extras, where not fitted as standard, included air-conditioning, electronically controlled anti-lock braking system, heated front seats, heated front windscreen, and more.

PRICES (1993): Mondeo 1.6 saloon

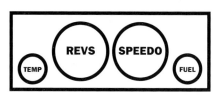

Instrument layout LX, GLX, Si, Ghia.

Gear change diagram.

£11,448, 1.8LX hatchback £12,637, 1.8 GLX hatchback £13,715, 2.0 GLX estate £14,900, 2.0 Si saloon £15,675.

COLOURS (1993): Diamond White, Garnet Red, Radiant Red, Isis Blue, Rimini Blue, Black, and metallics Stardust Silver, Levante Grey, Cayman Blue, Java Blue, Pumice Gold,

Estate Turbo diesels.

Nouveau Red, Coral Red, Alberto Green. Not all colours available for some models.

ENGINE (1993): Four-cylinder, petrol engines are DOHC with fuel-injection, EEC IV engine management system, electronic breakerless ignition and catalytic converter. 1.6i, bore 76mm, stroke 88mm, 1597cc (97.45in^3), maximum 90PS at 5250rpm; 1.8i, bore 80.6mm, stroke 88mm, 1796cc (109.6in^3), maximum 115PS at 5750rpm; 2.0i, bore 84.8mm, stroke 88mm, 1988cc (121.3in^3), maximum 136PS at 6000rpm; 1.8 diesel, bore 82.5mm, stroke 82mm, 1753cc (106.9in^3), mechanical fuel-injection system, maximum 88PS at 4500rpm.

ENGINE (1994): Six-cylinder, V formation, DOHC, bore 82.4mm, stroke 79.5mm, 2544cc (155.2in^3), maximum 170 PS at 6250rpm, multipoint fuel-injection system.

GEARBOX: Five-speed, all-synchromesh, floor-mounted gear change. Ratios: 1.6, 1.8 and 2.5 top 3.126, 4th 4.182, 3rd 5.887, 2nd 8.688, 1st 13.885, reverse 14.048 (2.5 14.697); 2.0 top 3.264, 4th 4.262, 3rd 5.683, 2nd 8.218, 1st 13.133, reverse 13.286; 1.8 diesel, top 2.720, 4th 3.573, 3rd 5.116, 2nd 8.323, 1st 14.859, reverse 14.048. Front-wheel drive, final drive ratio 1.6, 1.8 , 2.5 and 1.8 diesel 4.06:1, 2.0 3.84:1.

BRAKES: Dual-circuit, power-assisted, front

10.2in discs, rear 9in drums, ABS standard with Si and Ghia.

STEERING: Rack and pinion with variable ratio, power-assistance, safety steering column adjustable for reach and rake, anti-theft lock.

TYRES: Mondeo, LX, GLX, 185/65 x 14, Si 205/55 x 15, Ghia 195/60 x 14

SUSPENSION: Front, MacPherson struts, coil springs, anti-roll bar, rear Quadralink strut-type with coil springs, anti-roll bar. Estate models have different rear suspension incorporating short and long arms to reduce intrusion into the load space.

DIMENSIONS: Saloon **length**: 14ft 8.4in (4.48m); **width**: 5ft 8.9in (1.75m) or 6ft 3.8in (1.925m), with mirrors; **height**: 4ft 8.3in (1.43m); **wheelbase**: 8ft 10.5in (2.705m); **track**: front 4ft 11.25in (1.505m), rear 4ft 10.5in (1.485m); **ground clearance**: 4.7in (12cm); **turning circle**: 35ft 9.6in (10.9m). Hatchback as saloon except **height**: 4ft 8.1in (1.425m). Estate as saloon except **length**: 15ft 2.3in (4.63m); **height**: 4ft 8.7in (1.44m); **track**: rear, 4ft 11.25in (1.505m).

APPROXIMATE WEIGHTS: Saloon 1.6LX 1ton 3cwt 3qtr 19lb (1215kg), 1.8GLX 1ton 4cwt 1qtr 18lb (1240kg), hatchback 1.8GLX 1ton 4cwt 3qtr 6lb (1260kg), estate 1.6LX 1ton 4cwt 17lb (1265kg), 2.0 Ghia 1ton 6cwt 1qtr 5lb (1335kg).

CAPACITIES: Fuel 13.5 gallons (61.5 litres). Boot, saloon 17.09ft^3 (0.48m^3), hatchback 16.6ft^3 (0.47m^3), estate 19.8ft^3 (0.56m^3) or hatchback 45.9ft^3 (1.3m^3), estate 58.3 ft^3 (1.65m^3) with rear seat folded down.

Mondeo mark 1; later model with revised frontal treatment (all others are early models)

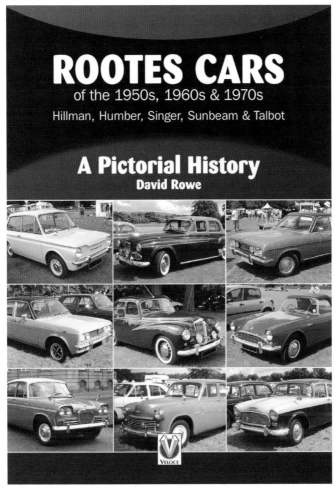

The only full-colour comprehensive guide to all Hillman, Humber, Sunbeam, Singer & Talbot cars and vans, from 1950 until the end of production in the 1970s. With model-by-model descriptions and detailed technical information, this is an invaluable Rootes resource.

ISBN: 978-1-787114-43-2
Paperback • 21x14.8cm • 168 pages • 1083 colour and b&w pictures

For more information and price details, visit our website at www.veloce.co.uk • email: info@veloce.co.uk • Tel: +44(0)1305 260068

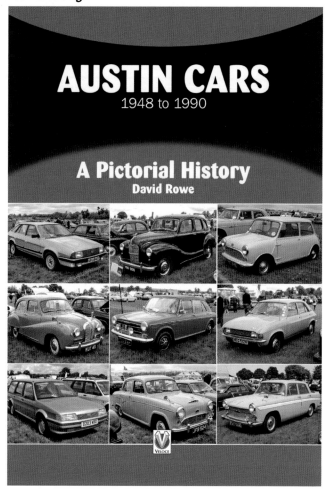

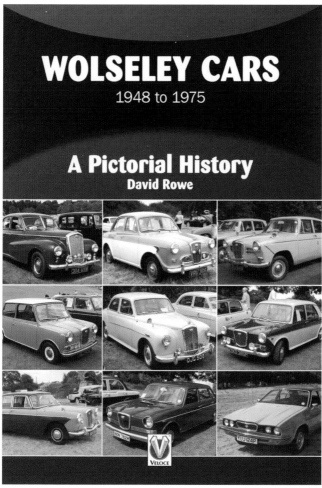

WOLSELEY CARS
1948 to 1975

A Pictorial History
David Rowe

A full-colour guide to all Wolseley cars built from 1948 until the end of production in 1975. With an informative history, detailed model-by-model comparisons and technical information, it is a comprehensive guide to the later cars.

ISBN: 978-1-787110-78-6
Paperback • 21x14.8cm • 80 pages • 300 pictures

For more information and price details, visit our website at www.veloce.co.uk •
email: info@veloce.co.uk • Tel: +44(0)1305 260068

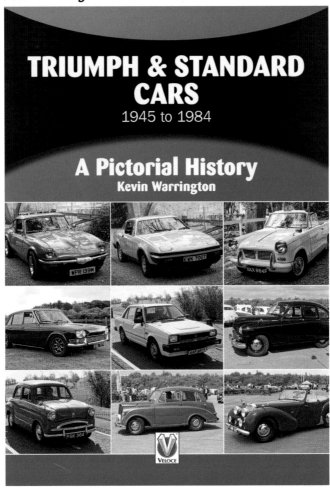

Index